"Cat Hulbert's lively tales from the table illustrate her expert advice with wit and candor and make for a highly entertaining, informative read."

—Toby Leah Bochan, author of
The Badass Girl's Guide to Poker

"With a light-hearted tone, Hulbert offers up strategies that will help anyone become a winning player."

—Barry Greenstein, high-stakes player
and author of *Ace on the River*

Outplaying the Boys

Outplaying the Boys

Poker Tips for Competitive Women

by Cat Hulbert

WORKMAN PUBLISHING NEW YORK

Published simultaneously in Canada by Thomas Allen & Son Limited.

Design by Paul Gamarello

Library of Congress Cataloging-in-Publication Data

Hulbert, Cat.

Outplaying the boys : poker tips for competitive women : why to check-raise whiners, bluff the pros, sweet-talk daddykins, and 117 other winning strategies / Cat Hulbert.

p. cm.

ISBN-13: 978-0-7611-3980-5 (alk. paper)

ISBN-10: 0-7611-3980-X (alk. paper)

1. Poker for women. I. Title.

GV1252.W66H85 2005

795.412'082--dc22

2005043683

Workman books are available at special discounts when purchased in bulk for premiums and sales promotions as well as for fund-raising or educational use. Special editions or book excerpts can also be created to specification. For details, contact the Special Sales Director at the address below.

Workman Publishing Company, Inc.
708 Broadway
New York, NY 10003-9555

www.workman.com

Printed in the U.S.A.

First Printing September 2005
10 9 8 7 6 5 4 3 2 1

For Jon and Nicole Ungar

My generous sponsors who placed a big bet on the Undercat

Acknowledgments

This book brought to you with the generous assistance of:
Thomas Keisler, my trampoline for clear thinking
Robyn Joy Leff, my hero in all types of weather
Pat Lohr-Williams, my wise word processor

With the accumulation of knowledge from some very big brains:
David Heyden, a gifted guru of poker who combines fierce competition with kindness
Michael Michalek, the most original character in fact or fiction
Linda Ryke Drucker, who improves my being by simply being
Jimmy Warren, who always challenges me and himself

In existence because of the creative molding of my editor:
Margot Herrera

Conceived from the ego of a funny girl: Janet Carpenter

With the shared talents of my UCLA writing group, who all belong on a bookshelf:
Pat Lohr-Williams, Sharon Holmin, E. John Trewhitt, Scott Silva-Edwards, Ann Boehmer, Robyn Joy Leff, Roark Harlan Whitehead

With much appreciation to my first writing teacher: Phyllis Gebauer

Indebted to Richard Munchkin, author of *Gambling Wizards*

An overture of gratitude to Dr. Wes Burgess for his dedication to a healthy mind

A sweet kiss of appreciation to Deborah Elliot, founder of Poker Night 4 Girls—But you'll have to come home to get it

Thanks to Alex Outhred for World Poker Tour research assistance

All-weather IOUs to my best buds:
Craig Chellstorp, who will be the subject of my next book—*From Chess Champion to Ballroom Dancer*
Jeff Stauter, the good-natured butt of many a life anecdote
Linda Stein, who thinks the red-ribbon prize is just toilet paper
Bonnie Costello, who takes big risks (and always lands on her feet)
Linda Stiefel, who is more colorful than a kaleidoscope

And with the hopeful longing that my treasured mama bear, Helen Hulbert, *will be proud.*

Contents

INTRODUCTION

Why you can trust me more than your car mechanic.

If I were a contestant on *Jeopardy!* and Alex Trebek announced the categories in the order of *Blackjack*, *Poker*, *Potent Potables*, *Big Dogs*, and *Chauvinistic Men*, you could bet your plasma television I'd win the first round. Of course, I'd never get to buzz in once if the categories were *English Monarchs*, *Cooking*, *Foreign Films*, *Economics*, and *Golf Legends.*

I know what I know, and as Thoreau said, that is true knowledge. Trust me, in the world of competitive poker, I started at the top, toppled to the bottom, and climbed back to the peak and planted my flag permanently. Because of my hard-won experience, I can show you how to stay away from both opponent *and* self-made traps, how to avoid belly-flop embarrassment, and how to employ trickery to win the chips. I understand the pitfalls because I've broken free of every trap imaginable, short of gnawing off my foot. I've learned how to overcome disaster and become a successful professional by self-honesty; by determination, resilience, and drive; by soaking up knowledge like a greedy sponge; and, last but not least, by pure luck. (No one will tell you it's against the law to get lucky.)

My gambling career started at the age of 24 when I left my press job at the New York State Senate, packed up my Honda nicknamed Blue, withdrew all my savings ($1,600), and drove head-on into Ohio's biggest snowstorm in 30 years. That's not necessarily the luckiest start, but I did meet a Lay's Potato Chips trucker while snowbound, who helpfully gave me the advice that I'd never make it in Vegas because my legs were too chunky.

But I wasn't on my pilgrimage to Vegas to be a showgirl; my quest was to be a professional card player.

What were my chances in 1976? In a well-read blackjack book of the time, the author flatly stated that a woman doesn't have the emotional fortitude to become a winning gambler. I had so many emotions in my youth that I could have built Fort Ticonderoga with them. And emotions aren't necessarily a bonus when monetary fluctuations can make you feel like you're going over Niagara Falls in a wooden barrel. (By the way, the first person brave enough for that daredevil stunt was a 63-year-old schoolteacher named Annie Taylor.)

In a well-read blackjack book, the author flatly stated that a woman doesn't have the emotional fortitude to become a winning gambler.

GETTING STARTED

Any man would have laughed his toupee off at the prospect

of me becoming a player and suggested I become a blackjack dealer or a cocktail waitress in a long skirt. But being a blackjack dealer is not being a *player*, which I quickly discovered when I got a job at the Rainbow Club in Henderson, Nevada, a suburb of Las Vegas. Bad luck befell me on the second day. The Rainbow Club changed its policy from the standard unisex dealer attire of black pants and a white shirt to cheek-high hot pants for the women. I resisted on feminist grounds, but the real reason for my protestation was my linebacker gams. Twenty-four hours later I quit my first casino job on "moral grounds."

My next job was spinning the Big Six Wheel at the Union Plaza Casino in downtown Vegas, and two months later I moved up to dealing blackjack. It wasn't long before I began to discern that there were some true pros at the game. I wanted—no, I needed—to know their secrets.

One day a pro who looked like Sonny Bono wearing a fake Versace shirt came in, and I finally asked, "What's your system?" He looked startled and whispered back, "Shhh, meet me after work for coffee and I'll tell you."

At the time, I didn't even know such a thing as "card counting" existed, but I was about to get an up-close-and-personal education in it. Sonny Bono and I began dating, and he concocted a plan to teach me. He thought a woman card counter would be the greatest camouflage of all—simply because no one would ever suspect she'd be intelligent enough to use a system. What was wrong with the plan was that his team members thought having a female team member was as enticing as a skunk in a perfume shop. But Sonny persisted, and because he was the cash man and the team leader, the rest of the players begrudgingly fell in line. I kept

He thought a woman card counter would be the greatest camouflage of all—simply because no one would ever suspect she'd be intelligent enough to use a system.

practicing and practicing counting, sizing up how many cards were left in the deck, and dividing the remaining cards into the count.

At first, card counting seemed tough, owing to dividing fractions quickly, although now I think I could teach Koko the gorilla how to do it. It doesn't require mathematical genius, but rather the discipline to always follow the formula, to bear up under casino scrutiny, and to socialize and look like a tourist while simultaneously keeping rows of rapidly changing numbers in your brain. Maybe I am overestimating Koko, but the point is that you don't have to be a member of Mensa to count cards.

Because, as a woman, my abilities were still under suspicion, I was never allowed to bet the money, so my main function was as a spotter. A spotter acts anonymously, betting small and signaling the Big Player into the game when the deck becomes rich in high cards. She or he then passes the Big Player the count and disappears into the sea of faces. Was I frustrated because the team members wouldn't give me a chance to play solo due to my gender? Frustrated isn't the word; piping-hot mad is more apt. All I wanted was the chance to prove myself competent to play under pressure. But no one had ever heard of a female card counter. Plus Vegas in the '70s wasn't exactly the equal-rights capital of the world. So without seeming self-congratulatory, I think for overcoming these chauvinistic attitudes and pioneering the way for other female players that I deserve a Benny Goodman toot or two.

As a member of Sonny's team, I traveled all over Europe, Asia, and Australia counting cards and slowly accumulating a bankroll. I was sharp and tough, and gradually gained the respect of my teammates because I could shove the money out without fear when the count called for it. Often people believe that's what divides the girls from the boys in gambling—how they handle fear. And although men think they are the braver of the two genders, it's not necessarily true. Woman guts and man guts look the same during an autopsy, and I would die trying to prove myself as a competitive equal. Well, maybe not on all fronts—I'm still happy I never got a draft lottery number.

FROM BLACKJACK TO POKER

Even though I became an infamous player, barred on sight from casinos in such exotic places as Macau and Katmandu, my main desire was still to become a poker player. After 12 years on the blackjack circuit, I quit. I was tired of being backroomed by casinos, of facing hostility from dealers and pit bosses, of sitting in holding cells on trespassing charges, of always being on the road, and of living in constant fear of getting robbed. So I took a stab at making my first dream a reality.

How hard could it be to make the transition from blackjack to poker? They are both card games, right? Wrong! In poker, you can teach someone how to play a particular hand, but it's like chess—there are countless variations of the same situation that can occur and numerous levels of judgment that need to be plugged in. But even more than the complexities of the game, my main stumbling blocks were my confrontations with other players. Blackjack was just *me* against the house, but poker came with personalities that ranged from racist scumbag to snake-like vermin.

I turned into a sucker, avoiding the truth, playing in the highest games with guys who could play rings around me.

And if I thought I'd faced chauvinism in the blackjack world, I discovered that I hadn't scraped the surface of how threatened a competitive man can be by an aggressive and strong-willed woman. Instead of just thinking their thoughts or expressing grumbles of dissatisfaction, some male poker players try to verbally pick you apart like vultures.

Although I believed I would be oblivious to the attacks because I was a hotshot blackjack player, I turned into a vulnerable woman. At a time when I should have been concentrating on my game, I was perfecting my bantering techniques. I turned into a sucker, avoiding the truth, playing in the highest games with guys who could play rings around me. And instead of being focused on making money, I was concerned with winning the battle of the sexes. I lost badly, and the pain of crying into my pillow each night took its toll on my psyche, bankroll, and—even worse—my great-looking face. Safe to say, Benny put his clarinet down and took a long break.

CHANGING MY TUNE

How did I turn things around? Well, I swallowed my pride, dropped down to the small games, found a great poker teacher who forced me to face my weaknesses, and mastered the secrets of the founding principles of poker.

Now, I *love* poker—85 percent of the time I'd rather be playing than shopping at Nordstrom (and I'm a shopaholic!). If you are a woman who's been nibbled by the gambling bug, whether it's a pastime or a professional pursuit, I can turn your curiosity into knowledge. But there will still be those days Mama didn't tell you about, and that's why I'm here to guide you past your ego and any personal weakness that may hinder your growth as a player. Poker is exhilarating when you win, and you can handle that side of it standing on your head. But when you lose, it's a test of character.

I have taught poker to women for several years, and through my own roller-coaster ride and through my interactions with my students, I understand where the traps lie for the novice. I can show you how to navigate around them and not get lost in the sea of wannabe players.

One dangerous pitfall is not being prepared to play against men who cannot stand losing to the weaker sex. Those men believe that because their muscular development is superior to ours, so is their psychological advantage. (Of course, it's more than muscle; it's also societal and cultural indoctrination.) I know how to demolish that archaic belief by introducing you to ways that will strengthen your advantages and diminish your weaknesses. The truth is our gender *does* tend to suffer particular weaknesses, but if we acknowledge them, we can implode them.

Poker is exhilarating when you win. But when you lose, it's a test of character.

It's my firm belief that if you build a sturdy foundation of what you need to know to become a winner, you can then use your natural advantage of being female to finish the race miles ahead of your male opponents. (And it's no coincidence that the finish line is at the door of your local bank.)

Poker for me is a way to strengthen the areas that I am weak in, develop my analytical abilities, improve my memory, and compete against men in a way I never can when physical strength is an issue. I've written 117 essential tips with accompanying explanations and life anecdotes that will build the necessary springboard for the beginner and increase the skill level of the experienced player.

The poker novice is not expected to understand every lesson, but eventually her knowledge will catch up with her experience and that 40-watt light bulb will start beaming like a lighthouse in the fog.

One of the downfalls of the experienced player is that she becomes satisfied with her game. She stops trying to learn and expand her capabilities. When you are a beginner, everything seems new and you're open to new tactics, but a player who becomes complacent will not notice the gradual decay of her game as bad habits become ingrained and opportunities go by unseen. This book is equally valuable for players of all levels.

THE POKER GAME OF LIFE

It's my hope that these poker tips will improve your game and have applications beyond the green felt table. My ideas on how to handle a wide spectrum of men—from the chauvinist to the pussycat—may apply to women in any male-dominated workplace or setting, from the corporate boardroom to the tennis court. You can operate—"act like a man"—but still think like a woman without being seen as a witch-on-wheels (or worse). Using my techniques, you can reframe the picture of feeling like the odd woman out because you'll discover there are secret advantages to being female in almost every venue—well, at least those that don't involve one-armed pull-ups.

Poker is the hottest game in the country, and everyone from trendy celebrities to suburban moms is after the thrills of a winning hand, whether they're playing at home, in a casino, or on the Internet. This quick-moving game of skill has long been a "boy's night" staple, but here's the truth: The fastest-growing segment of poker players today is women. Some are taking up the game seriously with the goal of becoming a professional player, and other girls are Cyndi Lauper fans—they play just to have fun. I attend regular friendly home games—some gender-mixed, some all-women—because they are social outlets where I can laugh, relax, gossip, and interact without any underlying motivation but enjoyment.

Whatever our purpose for playing, let's all celebrate together when the first woman wins the World Series of Poker. The celebration may be followed by a funeral, because old-timer Thomas "Amarillo Slim" Preston said he'd kill himself if that ever happened. Slim, what's your pleasure—pistol or poison?—because you can bet a woman will capture the title. The only question is, will she do it before or after a female lands in the Oval Office?

I plan on sharing two of my other areas of *Jeopardy!* expertise by finishing my book on big dogs and L.A. bartenders in time for a Christmas 2005 release, so keep an eye out for it.

If you fell for that bluff, you definitely need to keep reading *Outplaying the Boys*!

—Cat Hulbert

1

Getting to First Base on the First Date

What You Need to Know and Think About Before You Start to Play

TIP 1

Understand your reasons for playing poker, but always try to win.

Ask yourself this simple question: Why are you playing poker? Is it because the season finale of your favorite sitcom has left you without a reason to live? (Poor thing, but September will be here soon.) Are you playing because that outrageously hot guy in 2B is always taking trips to the casino? (Honey, that man ain't worth it, but you might as well take his cash.) Are you playing because you know you're better, brighter, and ballsier than the rest? (If you think that, then you probably are.) Knowing your motivations for playing will help you focus on your strengths and improve on the areas in which you're weak. For example, if you realize that you're playing to prove to your ex-husband that you're not the passive patsy he claimed you were, then you might want to watch your tendencies to be overaggressive.

Whatever your reasons for playing—to escape, for the mental rush, to show off, for entertainment—let me add this: It's always more fun to be a winner than a loser, whether the payoff is $5 or a number with a whole bunch more zeros. Approach the game as a means of increasing your income, whether it's the coins in your piggy bank or the cash in your safe-deposit box.

Most of all, you should play because winning enhances your self-esteem faster than a year's worth of psychotherapy.

Most of all, you should play because winning enhances your self-esteem faster than a year's worth of psychotherapy. If you can show me a woman who wouldn't benefit from another ounce of confidence, I'll point out that you're looking at a storefront mannequin.

TIP 2

Prepare yourself physically and mentally before entering the green-felt jungle.

When I first started playing poker, playing with the big boys literally meant playing with the *big* boys. Although it sounds catty, the majority of players were fat-fat or out of shape, lounging back in their chairs like polyester iguanas. Soothing an injured ego or unwinding after a taxing session wasn't done at 24 Hour Fitness; built-up stress was relieved by gobbling down two dozen mini White Castle hamburgers or rolling a log-sized doobie. These days there is a new breed of poker player who is bringing a new advantage to the game—fitness. Although playing poker certainly doesn't look as physically demanding as entering the ring with Marvin Hagler, sometimes it can be as energy-draining, especially when you're in a multiple-day tournament or in a downward spiral.

The better shape you're in, the more capable you are of withstanding the punch that comes from your opponent turning a **gut-shot straight***. Nowadays the young studs don't just want to win your money; they want to beat you out of it. How tough is it at medium and higher stakes? Put it this way: It makes taking a kindergarten class to Disneyland on the Fourth of July seem like a picnic. You are going to face a table of opponents whose main aim is to psychologically outwit you and find weaknesses in your game or character, and who will feel no remorse if you just lost little Johnny's Montessori tuition. Many of these cutthroats are ready to add any type of verbal humiliation that will unhinge you and make their job easier. It's called the green-felt jungle because the rules of survival of the fittest apply.

Unless you were born Xena, Warrior Princess, developing the traits necessary to play with expert men takes an unswerving passion and the willingness to pick yourself up

***Gut-shot straight—the making of a straight by catching a card inside the sequence. For example, if you draw 9-10-Q-K, the jack is the gut-shot.**

and try again over and over. Poker is tough, and because you're female, some of your male opponents are going to want to beat you so they can smugly maintain that worn-out stereotype that a woman belongs in the kitchen (or bedroom) and not in their private domain—the poker table.

KEEP A CLEAR HEAD

The second half of the equation (for many of the reasons I have just outlined) is having a strong, flexible, and resilient mind. Some days we are just off, and you have to recognize those times and avoid the battle. You can't be worrying about whether your husband is sleeping with Marcia or whether your daughter Cindy is sneaking Marlboros; your mind must be free of distracting clutter. The best way to keep a focused brain is to sleep regular hours. If you are a person who needs 10 hours of sleep, be sure you get it. A sleep-deprived mind has trouble isolating a problem under pressure, and poker requires rapid-fire decisions with a mapped-out strategy from your starting hand all the way to the **river***.

Likewise, a mind soggy from too many cocktails the night before will be at a disadvantage against the guy who chose carrot juice instead of Jell-O shots at midnight. A small leak can sink a great ship. We just don't know what is going to be in store for us when the session begins. Maybe we can trick fate occasionally, but even in a few sessions, the alert, calm, and patient mind champions over the luck factor.

Meditation is the perfect way to calm your brain before a session if you're feeling haywire. If you are too agitated to sit

***River—the seventh card dealt in seven-card stud. The fifth community card in Texas hold 'em.**

and breathe quietly for 20 minutes, you shouldn't be risking your money that day. If you're on the freeway feeling rage at the redneck who just cut you off, you shouldn't be playing poker either. If meditation isn't for you, develop your own methods for flattening out the rough edges before you play, whether it's a walk in the woods or a hot bath. You need to know your own mind and be honest with its daily fluctuations. Poker is a game that makes you want to jump out of bed and race into the poker room to get the next hand. It's soul-grabbing, but you have to fight the urge to go in unprepared.

TIP 3

Go for a look that conveys confidence and personal pride.

What have girls always been able to do better than boys (even the most arrogant fellow will admit it)? Dress ourselves without calling our mothers. (Of course, some of us do ask our gay friends if we look fat, but that doesn't count.) Clothes convey confidence, and confidence converts to dollars. Choose an outfit that makes you feel strong; something in which you feel comfortable, classy, and powerful. Your opponent doesn't have to know you've chosen an elastic waistband. (Those of us who have sat in size 8 jeans with a size 10 body for eight hours can vouch for comfort. We need to be able to focus only on the cards and not worry about whether we're going to suffocate to death in zippered denim.) And don't make your only pit stop your closet—spend some time in front of the mirror on your hair, and don't forget that your hands are always in the spotlight. You might not think men notice whether you're sporting a French manicure or fire-engine red polish, but they do—and a woman who cares about her appearance is more intimidating at the tables.

A CLASSY STYLE PROJECTS A DAUNTING TABLE IMAGE

Our ability as women to feel confident simply by looking good is one of our advantages. I don't understand why some women players pooh-pooh the notion. I have one poker-playing friend who is very pretty but dresses like a Salvation Army vagabond and always slouches down in her chair. Her reason is when she looks hot, all the guys try to hit on her and it's too distracting to her game. Though I don't think you have to look sexy, I do believe she is missing an opportunity for a knock-dead killer image. If she weren't so leery of confrontation, she could simply say, "Excuse me, I don't mix playing poker with pleasure and don't talk at the table," or "My husband is a cop and prefers that I don't date."

If sexy is your *natural* style and you're not afraid of offending the feminists, flaunt it. Most poker boys, young and old, are hound dogs, and they won't be able to remember the

> "I have heard with admiring submission the experience of the lady who declared that the sense of being perfectly well-dressed gives a feeling of inward tranquillity that religion is powerless to bestow."
>
> —Ralph Waldo Emerson

color of their money if they see a perky nipple or a hint of cleavage.

If you look like you take pride in yourself, you'll feel like a winner, and people will react to your bets differently than if you look anonymous and mousy. Players will be more fearful of you and less apt to raise you. At the onset of a hand, thoughts of how much is this going to cost me will go through your opponent's head. Men will respect your aggression more, and you'll be more likely to bluff them.

I'm not saying try to be someone you're not. Take your own look and choose whatever outfit you feel best in. Think about what you'd like to be wearing if you ran into an old rival from school or work—someone you haven't seen in years. Go for a look that says, "I'm strong, I'm happy, and nobody can knock me off my pedestal."

Take a Cue from Cyndy

One famous female player who works her image to the hilt is Cyndy Violette. Her style is completely the opposite from mine—she's a petite sprite, whose look says "little sister." Cyndy wears cut-off jean shorts, a brightly colored T-shirt, and a baseball cap backward that spells "I'm so cute you wouldn't dare raise me." Men want not only to take her out for an ice-cream soda but also to check rather than bet on the river. Her opponents' mistaken idea that she is just an innocent little girl enables Cyndy to use her skill as a player to reel in the **fish***. (Another thing she does right is dress in layers. Often poker rooms turn hot or cold very quickly, and being able to adjust to the climate change is important.)

***Fish—the sucker in the game; he who is unskilled, naive and thus the target of the better players.**

In my case, my penchant for the color pink creates an unsettling contradiction of images. What men see is an aggressive woman, an outspoken woman, a woman unafraid of conflict, but she's wearing baby-girl pink. To be able to confuse your opponent by style versus presence is another way to take advantage of the male stereotype of woman and throw him off guard.

Our ability as women to feel confident simply by looking good is one of our advantages.

Don't underestimate those guys wearing 10-year-old baseball caps. They do know the difference between a woman who has style and one who would make Blackwell's Worst-Dressed list. Your goal at the poker table is to always be the player who controls the action, and if you start off with a winning image, you've overcome one of the hurdles to finding your place in a male-dominated environment.

TIP 4

Be aware of how your opponents perceive you.

Consider this scenario: Charles, a businessman, is going 75 mph on the freeway when his tire blows. He's late for a meeting, and his head was so scrambled when he left the house, he forgot his cell phone. Chuck gets out of the car and looks helplessly at the tire—he doesn't know the difference between a lug nut and a tire wrench. He begins to panic, but then a young blond woman dressed in a skirt and heels pulls up in a fancy Corvette. She offers assistance, and Charles is embarrassed but asks if she knows how to change a tire. She removes her Armani jacket, walks to the dash, pops the trunk, then proceeds to jack up the car. An 18-wheeler whooshes by and the trucker blasts his horn. What is Charles thinking? What is the woman thinking?

The purpose of this exercise is to show how every day in ordinary circumstances we size up others as they size up us. Women tend to be more interested in the image they project because, hell, most of us spend five times as long as men preparing to leave the house for work. We want to create a positive impression and premeditate how to achieve the best effect. We're practiced, so the leap to the poker table isn't much more than a wide step.

Let's consider another example: You sit down at a seven-card stud poker table in a new casino, and seven pairs of eyes watch and seven minds wonder. You are wearing a tan cashmere sweater, Versace silk scarf, tight jeans, and high-heeled boots. Your left hand is decked out with your new 3-carat engagement ring. You're feeling confident; you bought in for double the buy-in and have more chips than anyone at the table. Your opponents are regular Joes, except for the gentleman in the No. 2 seat wearing a Hugo Boss suit with a gold Rolex watch. He flashes you a smile. The action begins, and you look down and find a pair of kings; Hugo has a queen up and raises. The other players fold and now it's up to you. You reraise. What is Hugo thinking?

You can bet your Manolo Blahniks that Hugo is going to feel a sting. If he has any pair, he's going to reraise you. He may even reraise with three random cards. He feels he's the only one who extended any type of warmth to your arrival, and you immediately dishonored this courtesy. Watch his face very carefully, because you're going to be able to tell a lot from his expression. Men in suits at a poker table are usually casual players and unpracticed in hiding emotion. He has no information about whether you're an aggressive player or simply a loose one. But he is going to want to see what you're holding even if he has to chase you to the river with a knowingly inferior hand. On sixth street he **check-raises*** you, and it's not obvious his hand has improved. You reraise and he raises you right back—his chips splash with anger into the pot. On seventh street he bets. What do you do? If you had prior information about this player, such as the fact that he always has the goods, you could easily fold if you have not made two pair. But you don't know him, and he doesn't know you, and you have the male/female factor to consider. You have to gain your own starting information, so you definitely would want to see his hand. You call. He smugly shows you three concealed deuces. The information you gather is this:

1. Hugo was playing a poor-quality starting hand by raising **under the gun**** with a pocket pair of deuces. He's very loose and aggressive.
2. He was trying to push you around by his check-raise on sixth street, hence you made a good play by reraising.

*Check-raise—at his turn a player checks hoping a later-positioned opponent will bet. When the action gets back to the checker, he then raises.
**Under the gun—refers to the first position to act after the low card in stud or the first position to act after the big blind in hold 'em.

3. The other six players at the table have all been watching. They will be dying to know what you are holding. Of course you don't show. Restrain yourself from giving any type of defeatist reaction. What the other players have also gleaned is that you are not going to be easily run over by a reraise and you're not going to be easily bluffed on seventh street.

From just one hand you have learned a tremendous amount about one opponent, and Hugo and the other six players have learned a tremendous amount about you. Anyone who plays the next hand with you will know you're aggressive, fearless, and not easily bluffed.

The way he perceives you affects whether a man will play dirty, overplay his hand, play softly, or avoid you like a black widow spider.

Don't forget, the image you project can change rapidly depending upon many factors. A foreseen example: how you act when you lose a hand, whether you wing the cards and curse the dealer, or tap the table and politely say, "Nice hand." An unforeseen example: You obviously have just received bad news via your cell phone—do you lose focus or are you able to stay with the task at hand?

Players evaluate other players without even realizing they are doing it. The difference between you and the average player is that you're going to learn to anticipate and assess your opponent's perception of you. When you are in the midst of chip fire, you'll have a factor in the equation that he does not. You can't always predict what will happen, but you can always analyze the effect it had at the conclusion.

2

How to Wear Basic Black to Stay out of the Red

Laying an Indispensable Foundation for Safeguarding Your Bankroll

TIP 5

Play with a predetermined bankroll stop-loss.

During a boxing match, the boxer can depend upon his ringside coach to throw in the towel if his eyeball is hanging out of its socket. The coach doesn't confer with the boxer first because the boxer's mentality is that he won't stop throwing punches until he's unconscious. In poker none of us wants to stop when we're losing either, but we don't have an adviser with a towel ready to flip into the air. It's up to us to be emotionally stable enough to determine when we should call it quits for that session.

A few poker experts believe you should not play with a **stop-loss*** if there still is easy money to be made and you're in control. I contend that when you are losing, your capacity to determine whether you are still playing a winning game is highly questionable. I've played with a couple of these poker experts who disagree, and I've watched them turn from heavyweights into 98-pound weaklings. As your chip stack

***Stop-loss**—a predetermined maximum amount you are willing to lose in a session.**

dwindles, your image turns sour and more players will attempt to outplay you (and usually succeed). Factors you could count on when you were perceived as a winner are now fluctuating. Even the producer at the table will be eyeing you as an investor for his next film.

DON'T SECOND-GUESS YOURSELF WHEN IT'S TIME TO TOSS IN THE TOWEL

I wish I could give you an exact amount as to when to quit at several game limits, but it is different for each person depending upon her discipline level. From experience, I know exactly when my judgment becomes flawed and I rely on a calculation of 50 top bets. Until you decipher for yourself when your reality becomes distorted by getting clobbered from losing, you can use my figures. So if you are playing $2/$4, 50 top bets is $200. At $5/$10, 50 top bets is $500; at $15/$30, 50 top bets is $1,500; and at $40/$80, 50 top bets is $4,000.

If you find yourself desperately pleading for someone to cash a check or waiting in line at the ATM machine for a third time, your brain is suffering from a lack of oxygen. Try to remember the last time you needed to make a logical decision while you were in emotional turmoil. How'd that work out for you?

I'd like to bet that if you get a series of Pow! Pow! Pow! **bad beats***, you're going to start to reel. If the loss begins to add up to an amount that makes you feel as if someone were holding your head underwater, overwhelming and impossible to comprehend, you've hit your stop-loss.

***Bad beat—a strong hand beaten by an improbable one.**

Believe me, even if you're smart enough to set a predetermined stop-loss, as you close in on that limit the devil will start whispering in your ear: "But the fish still has a stack of hundreds! You're the best player in the game. Even if you make a few mistakes, you still have positive expectations. Are you a quitter? Quitters are losers, Missy!"

"Well, to make a fair bankroll short, it don't take me long to learn about the game."

—Will Rogers
"A Visit to Monte Carlo"
A Will Rogers Treasury

Regarding the last excuse, the devil's salary is paid by that type of thinking. Players who know when to quit have a starting edge against any player who does not. You'll quickly be able to determine whether you have the discipline to be a consistent winner by seeing whether you are capable of adhering to a stop-loss limit. Of course it's not easy—and that's why "show discipline and restraint" has been No. 1 on my New Year's resolution list for the last 20 years.

TIP 6

Keep simple notes on the playing habits of your opponents.

You gather important information as you play, so record it. Don't rely on your recollection; taking notes helps cement opponents' playing characteristics into your memory. It's worth the effort when you're a beginner to catalog this information. [Most intermediate players think they are above taking notes (but aren't), and advanced players usually have mastered the skill of committing opponents' playing habits to memory.]

We don't always know our opponents' names, so give each a catchy nickname that reflects the player's most distinctive trait. Many people in the poker room go by nicknames anyway. Some of my favorites are:

The Weaver. *Reason:* He likes to weave a web of controversy between two players, and then step back and watch the fireworks.

Psycho Steve. *Reason:* Occasionally, for no determinable cause, he shifts out of stability into insanity in less time than it takes to shuffle the deck.

Suzie Cream Cheese. *Reason:* I'm not sure I know, other than it's a cute nickname and so is she.

Prince of Darkness. *Reason:* Whatever is about to happen, he expects it to be the worst possible scenario.

Mega. *Reason:* He is a megalomaniac. Interesting character actually. He could have been an inventor but instead uses his bizarre imagination to outwit casinos.

You get the idea. If a player makes a lot of chauvinistic comments, you have a choice of a dozen nicknames you could draw out of your thinking cap.

IDENTIFY CONSISTENT BEHAVIOR

One easy way to develop a database of opponents' playing traits is to take notes on a small pad that you keep out of sight at the table. But be subtle about it. There's nothing more dorky or open to sarcasm than some egghead scribbling away during a hand. (Of course, you can transfer these notes into a computer database when you get home.) Many players have habitual ways of playing a certain hand. If you can identify this consistent behavior, future playing decisions are as easy as dialing your best friend's phone number. Here's an example of some notes you might take:

Chip-Burner Charlie

- Raises with any pair from any position. Check-raises on the turn with flush draws.
- Bets sports simultaneously—**tilts*** when team loses. (Keep an eye out and an ear open.)
- High frequency bluffer—call, call, call.

Betty Boop

- Makes marginal calls with high cards.
- Excellent **card reader****.
- Extracts the maximum.
- Ask immediately how long she's played. Decision-making flawed on second day.
- Easily provoked. Keep mouth shut.

The Producer (Every card club in L.A. will have at least three. The only time it's actually his profession is when you don't know it.)

- Plays every hand.
- Raises only when he's made a hand the first two hours. After he's big-time stuck, turns erratic.

*Tilt—when an opponent goes emotionally off-kilter.
**Card reader—good card readers can accurately estimate an opponent's holding.

- Has a stop-loss of 6K.
- Will leave if he wins 2K in the first hour.
- Very fragile ego. Keep it jovial.

ESSENTIAL INFORMATION

The key points you'd like to know about each player are:

1. What is the quality of his starting hand (solid, marginal, horrific)?
2. Does he fast-play or slow-play a high pair?
3. Does she check-raise with or without the **nuts***?
4. Does she **raise on the come****?
5. Can he analyze a player's hand correctly? What grade would you give him regarding his card-reading abilities: A, B, C, D, or F?
6. Does she tilt? At what point?

If you think you're a smarty, just try going around a table of regulars and asking yourself questions No. 1 through No. 6. If you fall short of knowing the answers, you're not working hard enough.

*Nuts—a hand that cannot be beaten at that point.

**Raise on the come—for example, in hold 'em you have two spades as starting cards, and the flop contains two more spades. If you raise with the four-flush, it's called raising on the come, in hopes that the remaining card or cards will complete your hand.

TIP 7

Be realistic about your skill level when selecting a game.

Ask me whether I know a professional poker player who doesn't think he's better than he actually is, and I'll answer, "Nope." At some point in each gambler's life, he has played in a game with a negative win rate, either because he was outclassed, being cheated, or needed to lie in wait for a **pigeon*** to land. If he was outclassed, pride or arrogance could be responsible; if he was being cheated, it's because of unfortunate ignorance; if he was lying in wait for a pigeon, sometimes good players are willing to (and often should) take a temporary downside to get the game started.

When you have the opportunity to select your game, you want to be honest about your skill level and not sit down at a table where the players are ready to swallow you whole because they've got more money, talent, and experience. Sometimes you are not privy to this information until after you've plunged into the game. But shortly thereafter, you should evaluate honestly whether you're in over your head, and if you are, you must find a new beach that isn't shark-infested.

***Pigeon—a very weak player.**

FIND A BALANCE

The best type of game for most players, beginners and advanced alike, is one that's divided half-and-half into thinking and **maniac*** players. Why? Because having a few thinkers provides balance and eases fluctuations. And maniacs just lose, making the game more profitable for you. When you are learning, you want to try to adapt the principles you are acquiring. If seven players call your raise when you're holding aces, the likelihood of your winning without improvement is less than 25 percent. In a wild game such as this, the best starting hand frequently doesn't hold up and you're going to have higher fluctuations. It's also frustrating to be denied the satisfaction of playing as well as you know how and not reaping the financial benefits quickly. (Of course, what you must realize is that when you do improve your hand, the pots will be larger and will make up for those unfortunate times you lose, lose, lose with your high pairs.) Finally, card reading almost becomes impossible in a game where eight players are constantly calling, and as a beginner you want to hone that particular skill.

> "Talent makes its own luck."
>
> —William Kennedy
> *Billy Phelan's Greatest Game*

If you find yourself in a game of maniacs where everyone is playing like a monkey and treating his money like bananas, be prepared for some wild swings. It can be stressful if your bankroll is tighter than King Kong's chokehold. If this is unnerving, consider bowing out and finding a more stable game with fewer crazies and lower fluctuations. But don't be silly enough to say the game is unbeatable because

***Maniac—a player who bets, raises, and reraises without any regard to the quality of his hand.**

the monkeys didn't know a flush from a straight. In the long run, the worse your opponents play, the more bananas you will harvest. Just try to avoid falling into the trap of "monkey see, monkey do."

TIP 8

Consider the size of your bankroll in choosing the limit you play.

A bankroll's function is to supply you with enough playing capital to reduce the chances of ending up out of action. Your skill level and attitude are two keys to figuring out how many **units*** you need in your bankroll. Let's start with skill level. This isn't always easy to determine. If you're playing against three blind mice, you're an expert, but if you're facing seven dwarfs all wearing tournament gold rings, you're more likely to be paying for Snow White's new washer and dryer. But even if we don't always know who we'll be playing against, we still have to give ourselves some type of realistic skill label. If you are usually the best player in the game, you need fewer units because skill

***Unit—the size of the biggest bet in a limit game.**

increases your long-run chances for winning. If you are usually somewhere in the middle of the talent range, you will need more betting units.

What if your attitude is capricious and you just want to take a shot in the big game for the thrill of it? Sometimes that makes sense if you're not a **grinder*** and it doesn't matter if you're out of action in one session. After all, there's always the chance you'll win and never look back. Not a big chance, but a chance nonetheless, and that's why Las Vegas is overflowing with tourists who knowingly bet against the house advantage in pit games. If you're just playing for fun and a loss of capital won't mean an eviction notice on your front door, go for it! Nevertheless, what follows is for careful players who are OK with increasing their stakes slowly from the money they have put specifically aside for poker. (But not OK with going broke!)

> "'I hope I break even tonight,' was the sucker's philosophy. 'I need the money so bad.'"
>
> —Nelson Algren
> *The Man with the Golden Arm*

General rules of thumb:

1. If you are a novice, a 400-unit bankroll is suggested.
2. If you consider yourself an average player with at least 250 hours of playing experience, you'll probably be fine with 300 units.
3. If you are a very good player and have the records to prove it (more on this on page 34), 200 betting units should be sufficient.

***Grinder—a gambler who ekes out a living at small stakes.**

DON'T FLY KAMIKAZE MISSIONS WITH A SMALL BANKROLL

If you skid into a losing streak and your units are becoming burned rubber, drop down to a more comfortable limit to avoid going broke. Optimistically, you'll be a winner since you're interested enough to be reading this tip, and you can raise your stakes as your bankroll takes on some weight.

Look at this shoot-the-moon example for some perspective: Sally buys into a $3/$6 game for $30. (The minimum buy-in is always 10 times the lower figure.) She makes a big-grin win of $120 and decides to move up to the $15/$30 game (10 x 15 = $150). Once more Lady Luck touches Sally with her magic wand, and she does the Texas two-step to the cashier's cage. Day No. 3, she's already fantasizing about winning the World Series of Poker. She takes a seat in the $30/$60 game—and wins. Each time she wins, she elevates her game stakes and miraculously finds herself playing $300/$600. Oops, the first hand is a disaster. Her opponent makes two pair—deuces and fours—and beats Sally's aces. Game over. Sally is back handing out Happy Meals at the drive-thru at McDonald's. Did Sally get unlucky? Not if you understand that there was a 99-percent chance Sally would go broke before she reached the highest limit.

If Sally were mathematically prescient, she would have stopped at $15/$30 and padded her bankroll with enough units to stay in action. There are players who just want to take some extra cash and play poker. Fine and dandy, but instead of using a nice win to buy a bottle of Cristal to celebrate, the superior play is to quaff Perrier Jouët instead and put the rest of the money aside for a bankroll at reasonable stakes.

The gambling world has all kinds of stories about devil-may-care risk-takers. Stu Ungar is infamous for making and losing a million dollars over and over again. Some players walk a tightrope between fortune and ruin, and at least on the surface appear to have the psychological fortitude to handle stardom on Monday, and become a has-been on Tuesday.

A final point: You may have cashed out $1,500 at $15/$30 in one hour, but your win rate isn't $1,500 an hour. Win rates are calculated over the long run. One playing session is like a grain of sand on a 90-mile beach. I wouldn't presume to calculate a dependable win rate as a beginner before I had played 2,000 hours at a specific limit (which is realistically a year and a half of full-time effort).

Bottom line: Playing too high for your bankroll is very likely to lead to losing it, regardless of how good a player you might be.

Keep Your Poker Money Separate

It is important to keep your personal cash separate from your poker bankroll. As women, we may be more prone to mix our personal cash with our bankroll. At least half of us (according to another one of my surveys) sometimes spend money to make ourselves feel better, in the same way a person eats a hot fudge sundae as a substitute for love. We go shopping as part of a reward system for having a bad day, and it gives us a temporary high. Playing poker can supply the same high. It is crucial to understand that our bankroll is our means of continuing to invest in our game, and eventually to raise our stakes to a level at which a savings account becomes more attractive than a St. John's sweater.

TIP 9

If you have the choice, opt for a social, talkative game.

If you hear players laughing, even telling dumb blonde jokes, that's the game for you. (It's not my burden to defend; I'm a brunette.) A socially active game generally indicates that there are at least a few fat-wallet tourists who are playing just to have a good time, and they are going to be loose with their money, which means more profit for you (and more fun).

> "If you're in a card game and you don't know who the sucker is, you're it."
>
> —Anonymous Poker Saying

I know a few ornery stiffs who can't play against chatty players, and will even call the **floorperson*** over to try to get them to shut up. To those cranks I say, "Grow up!" Talking at a poker game can be used as a strategy to gain information on the strength of an opponent's hands or just to make the time waiting for a hand more interesting. Don't be a church mouse—add to the congeniality and you will get more action with your good hands.

***Floorperson—the casino employee who settles disputes and fields requests, such as getting a new deck or calling for a porter, security, or higher management.**

TIP 10

Do not multitask at the table.

I find it especially amusing when a player's chosen distraction is *Card Player* magazine. The funniest sight is to see a player entranced by an article in *Card Player* and not even know it's his turn. I have to hold my tongue from saying, "Did you see the article about always focusing on the action?" But I don't say a word, because a distracted opponent is a weak opponent.

If you're trying to learn the game while simultaneously flipping through catalogs or keeping an eye on the news on TV, poker just isn't for you. There are clues to a master puzzle popping up continually, and if you're reading "Dear Abby," you'll miss them (while she who's paying attention will not). My heart quickens when a player pulls up a seat and pulls a newsstand from his satchel. He's going to play A, B, C predictably. When suddenly *Scientific American* becomes less interesting to him than his cards, bingo, no surprise, he has a good hand. It's the same when someone is eating at the table. If he stops mid-bite to raise his **door-card*** king, throw your pair of jacks confidently into the muck.

***Door-card—the third-street-exposed card in stud.**

KEEP YOUR EARS OPEN

Another sight that makes me chuckle is serious players wearing headphones. They think it gives them an aloof appearance and will keep them detached and out of the line of verbal fire. Is that the image you want at a poker table—deaf and aloof? A player wearing headphones just doesn't understand how controversy among players affects the action. If you have just overheard Sam tell Harry he's going to raise his ass the next hand, you aren't going to get stuck in the middle with marginal cards. But if you have a big hand, you can **slow-play*** because Sam isn't going to miss a bet, and you can make a surprise pounce out of the bushes on a later street. You can't always rely on visuals, because plenty of people can maintain a deadpan expression but say something incendiary. What appears to be innocent conversation when you're sitting with your headphones on may actually be Harry threatening to let the air out of Sam's ego.

On the flip side, you also want to know when people are being friendly with one another, especially women and men. Is he annoyed she exists but making nice, or trying to pick her up? You need to understand all the motivations for player interactions at the table. And if you're the woman who is being chatted up, don't fall for any misleading patter because your heart is going a-pitter. Play your hand strongly, even if he looks like Denzel Washington and chuckles like George Clooney.

CELL PHONE EXPENSE

Ironically, your biggest enemy is the little item you charge every night and keep in your purse—your cell phone. Just

***Slow-play—when you don't raise with a powerful hand so as to trap other players.**

Never Miss Playing Poker on NFL Sundays

Although you don't want to allow distractions in your own game, you will relish them in your opponents'. My No. 1 favorite opponent is the weekend football fanatic or the horse handicapper. Missing the **pick six*** by one horse in the ninth race can throw a poker player's game off-kilter for days. Multitasking gambling because they can't get a big enough adrenaline rush from playing one game is a common male weakness (but some women are susceptible also). Such players are always going to be distracted and prone to tilt from disconnected events.

***Pick six—a jackpot pool with normally a huge payoff where you need to pick the winner of six consecutive horse races.**

when you are logically connecting the dots at the peak of concentration, brrriiing, Bach's "Fugue in D Minor" startles you, and the dots just blur. If you can, turn your cell phone off; if you must keep it on, screen your calls; if you have to answer, keep the conversation as short as possible.

TIP 11

Sit like a champion.

There is one psychological reason to sit up straight, with your feet planted squarely under your chair, and one physical one. Let's start with psychology. Who do you fear the most, the player who slumps or the one with the self-discipline to sit up straight? You will look more intimidating if you maintain proper posture. It's a little suggestion that can make a big difference to your table image.

The second reason is practical. Poor posture for hours on end will put stress on your vertebrae and throw your back out of alignment. It is very hard to play with a nagging backache, and continual visits to the chiropractor can take a chunk out of your bankroll. So do your body and your wallet a favor—and make your mother proud. Sit up straight.

TIP 12

Do not sit to the immediate right or left of the dealer if it's not for opponent advantage.

The most advantageous seat to sit in at a stud game is No. 2, and the second choice is No. 7. We have been brought up to believe that the most respected person at the dinner table sits at the head of the table. Sitting in the No. 2 seat gives you an automatic image of authority, as well as more table space and leg room. Moreover, it's disconcerting consciously or subconsciously for men to see a woman occupy the power position at a table. The least advantageous seats are No. 1 and No. 8, because if you're sitting in No. 1 you can't see the face of the player in No. 8, and vice versa. You miss out on all the opportunities associated with body language. Plus, the dealer may be more apt to sweep your cards into the muck if you fail to protect your hand.

In hold 'em, it's also wise to avoid the seats to the right and left of the dealer. The advantageous seats are Nos. 2, 3, 7, and 8. In both stud and hold 'em, seats No. 4 and No. 5 have their drawbacks, because as you peek at your pocket cards, it is easier for the players to your right and left to see your hand. So if those are your favorite seats, take extra care to conceal your hand. One sloppy peek and you can get burned by a big-eyed Looky-Lou.

All that said, sometimes the No. 1 or No. 8 seat (include No. 9 and sometimes No. 10 for hold 'em tables) is advantageous if you are seated to the right of the maniac. Being able to isolate the lunatic's hand and play **heads up*** is worth the sacrifice of missing out on a player's persona.

ON THE OTHER HAND . . .

At the risk of undoing everything I just told you, consider this (It will seem rather picky, but it's worth relaying because it once turned out to be a tournament bugaboo for me): Following my own advice, I always avoided the No. 4 and No. 5 seats because to memorize the cards that are out in stud, you have to turn your head from right to left. Because I successfully avoided those seats, I never became

***Heads up—when you play with a single opponent.**

accustomed to the visual process, and when I ended up with the luck of the tournament draw in seat No. 4, it felt like I was driving on the left side of the highway for the first time. Because there are times playing poker when you don't have a seat option, you do have an advantage if you are equally comfortable in each table position.

3

Mirror, Mirror, on the Wall, Why Aren't I the Fairest of Them All?

How to Avoid Self-Delusions

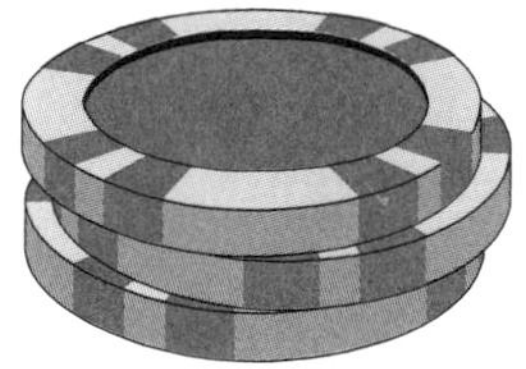

TIP 13

Keep detailed records of your wins/losses. Derive your hourly earn from reality.

You don't have to be a CPA to keep accurate playing records. My checkbook hasn't balanced in 20 years, but I can tell you whether I won or lost in July of 1991 without a smidgen of fudge. I am a firm believer in having concrete evidence on whether you're a winning or losing player. That's right; I don't trust your memory. Plus, why wouldn't you be tempted to stretch the truth a little—it's not going to hurt anyone, right? Wrong. It's going to skew the picture for the one person who needs to see it clearly—you. Records illustrate whether you're on the right path, need to get a new map, or maybe halt the trip altogether. If you're not a winning poker player after 2,000 hours of serious effort, it doesn't mean you're a bad person or a life loser, but it probably means you shouldn't refinance your house or break into your 401(k) for another bankroll infusion.

Poker is a trickster. It likes to pump your ego up one month and the next to make you wonder, if it weren't for bad luck, whether you'd have any luck at all. I can tell you that playing poker for a living is like boarding a roller coaster constructed by the devil. Of course, he's made it so addictively fun that you don't want to get off a loser—he's the devil after all. But it was an angel who first said, "Cut your losses!"

THE COLD HARD TRUTH

People choose to pamper delusions for many reasons. I have a buddy who has deceived himself his whole life about whether he can beat the track odds on horse racing. I occasionally ask him, "Don't you want to know whether you're a winner?" He answers, "No, because then I might have to give it up." So he persists in mixing his poker winnings and his horse losses, and is content to think he's a mediocre poker player (instead of excellent) but a halfway decent horse player (instead of not-so-good). When asked at the poker table, "Where do you live, Kenny?" he quips, "In the suburb of avoidance." There is no pain in his suburb, so you can see why it's such an attractive choice of location. But the catch is, only by facing the truth and being willing to feel the unpleasant sensations of being honest can you ever become a better player (or stop wasting precious time).

Because there are several different types of poker and various limits, it's beneficial to divide your records into categories. It does you little good to be a consistent winner in hold 'em if you sneak over to stud eight-or-better late at night because it's fun but you lose your skirt. The only way to diagnose a leak is by keeping accurate records of the games you've played, the limits, and the time spent at the table. Records can perform the specific functions of showing which game is your most profitable and which is your weak link. For example, you have been playing $15/$30 for more than a year with a win rate of $10 an hour, but look back and see that in a $10/$20 game your records show you made $15 an hour. You can see why dropping back to that level is the rational move.

Another benefit of record-keeping is that it reveals the freaky streaks of poker. There will be times when you want to swan dive off the Hoover Dam because you think you'll never win again, but if you look back at your records, they will help you remember that you thought you were invincible after winning 31 times in a row. Records keep the good times and the bad times in proper perspective.

TIP 14

If you experience too much fear, you are playing over your head.

There are things that scare me and things that don't. If I bumped noses with a shark while snorkeling, fear would propel my flippers back to shore as fast as the props of a 225-horsepower speed boat. Yet when I prepare to raise my opponent who has an NRA tattoo on a bulging bicep and a sneer on his face, I don't feel anything but focused anticipation. What's the worst that can happen? He raises me back. He's not going to pull out a rifle and shoot me for the grange hall's potluck dinner. Ask yourself when you start to experience panic at the poker table, "What's the worst that can happen?" You lose, you **muck***, the dealer shuffles, and another hand begins.

One reason I have an edge over my male opponents is that my fear factor at the table is bound to be less than theirs. Partly that's because it's in my basic personality to take risks, but I'm also convinced that I'm aided by cultural stereotypes. Boys are *supposed* to beat girls at every game and sport from Parcheesi to pole-vaulting. It's not an unjustified stereotype; we are divided into separate competitive fields in sports because of muscular differential, and although we can compete with men in chess and cards, many women still prefer the safety of same-sex competition. Men know this, so when a woman steps away from the stereotype, there is a caveman urge to put her back in her place. They can't use their fists or a bow and arrow, so they are going to look for subtle (or not so subtle) ways to intimidate women back into submission. About 35 percent of women will feel threatened when even a toothless geezer

"Fear is the main source of superstition, and one of the main sources of cruelty. To conquer fear is the beginning of wisdom."

—Bertrand Russell

***Muck** **1. (v) To throw your cards away: "I mucked the hand." 2. (n) The discards.**

mumbles, "There shouldn't be no damn females at a poker table." If this happens to you, simply smile and think to yourself, There shouldn't be any damn men who never brush their teeth. A second good response to a chauvinistic comment is to look straight at the speaker and laugh. Men who are irritated by a woman's presence at the poker table become unnerved when her response is laughter.

Remember, poker is an arena where you will get the upside from encountering chauvinism. Love thy chauvinist because it's he who will be paying for your pedicure.

Remember, poker is an arena where you will get the upside from encountering chauvinism. Love thy chauvinist because it's he who will be paying for your pedicure.

I don't have to get all stressed out when a man beats me, because that's the way he's always heard it should be. But if I beat a chauvinistic man, for him it's like a sandstorm in the desert. It's going to blind him with rage. As long as he believes my win is contrary to nature, I have the ultimate power even when I lose a hand.

Over the last 20 years, I've played with one narrow-minded man who would have had me stoned if we lived in the Middle Ages. If retreat is possible, he'll change tables when I sit down, but if he's stuck, or the fish is in our game, he'll begrudgingly squelch his aversion and play against me. His usual modus operandi is to play only monster hands with me, but sometimes he shifts gears and tries to bluff me. The only time I have to watch out for his bluffs is when he's so mad that he has turned fearless. It's easy to tell the difference between aggressive actions out of anger and tentative reactions out of fear. Anger is accompanied by a red face, sweating, and a haphazard crashing of chips into the pot. Actions arising out of fear lack a confident presence and are in slow motion. Ironically, when steam is coming out of his ears, he plays better because aggressive action is usually the correct play, but luckily 90 percent of the time he's just scared of me because I know his secret—he trembles from the fear of emasculation.

One way to control your heebie-jeebies is to have a big enough bankroll for the limit you are playing. I can admit that if I were to play a nitwit at stakes beyond my comfort level, I would feel as if I'd swallowed a carton of sea water each time I lost my kings to an inside straight. There goes

The Reverse Situation

I have one talented student who loses each time she plays low-stakes poker. She asked me why. I looked down at her $2,600 Prada bag and asked her, "What does winning sixty dollars mean to you?" She answered, "It's a round of drinks." I said, "That's your problem; you're playing too low. Raise your stakes until you get to the level where you do inhale when you lose a pot."

Your stakes can't be so low that the money is as meaningless as M&M's, but they can't be so high that each time you lose a pot it feels like Roger Clemens pitched a fastball into the side of your skull. Fear is part of poker, but your mission is to deal with your fear by trial and error, and to function within the parameters. Take solace, the 300-pound Hell's Angel across the table with the **short stack*** is feeling more fear than you.

***Short stack—a small stack of chips, usually because you're losing.**

the mortgage; there goes the tummy tuck; there goes my retirement in Costa Rica. There's a point for 99 percent of us when our formerly cavalier attitude toward the chips reverts to considering their purchasing power. That's the Peter Principle of poker—when we actually reach the level of our own incompetence and the beat of our heart is louder than an amplifier at a Smashing Pumpkins concert. So if you are feeling real fear, worse than finding your cat's eyes in your vichyssoise, cut the caboose loose and quit.

TIP 15

Do not play poker as a means of escaping your troubles.

One of poker's appealing qualities is that it can pull you out of daily life and transport you to a place where you don't think about anything but your next two cards. Or so we hope. The sad reality is, if you have an underlying problem, such as a broken heart, it will surface when you least expect it and botch up a hand. I have never known anyone, male or female, who can play at better than 70 percent of capacity when a thorn is lodged deeply in his or her brain.

On this issue I'm asking for your total trust. Do not play if you just put your pet to sleep, found out your husband has a second family in Idaho, were just disinherited by your father, caught your kid shoplifting, or flunked the bar exam for the third time. If anything has occurred that can bring a tear to your eye, stay out of the poker room and offline.

Do not play if you just put your pet to sleep, you found out your husband has a second family in Idaho, or you flunked the bar exam for the third time.

Poker is never going to provide the justice you think you deserve after one of life's hard knocks. It's only going to exacerbate the feeling of being out of control. I'm just guessing, but men may be less capable of avoiding poker during an emotional meltdown. They may fall victim to the familiar saying "Big boys don't cry" and thus be more apt to use poker as an escape.

There are times when I may make an assertion about gender that you'll quibble with. So I'll leave it up to you to decide (this time). Are women the more compassionate gender? And does this create a flaw in their game? My answers are yes and yes. How do you continue to extract money from a person you know is in emotional distress because life has given him a hard knock? First of all, you must remember that you're not responsible for his misfortune. Second, it's the cold part of poker, but if you don't play on and try to win his money, others at the table will. Third, if the circumstances were reversed, it's a rare individual who'll take you by the hand and lead you away from the table. Even if he's your best friend, his logic will be, If I don't take her money, someone else will.

And remember this: You'll definitely become very unpopular with the pros if you do decide to save a player on a day when he's feeling self-destructive. If you believe in free will, you need to respect the player's right to make a wrong choice.

HEARTBREAK IS GREAT FOR A DIET BUT CAN KILL A BANKROLL

I remember one time when the love of my life (LOML) broke up with me, and I used poker to escape my pain. I played all night, past my stop-loss limit, unknowingly trying to punish myself for a loss I had no control over. When the sun came up, the LOML appeared bright and chipper (damn him) and sat down at the table. There I sat, red-eyed, pathetic, with a two-inch stack of chips, which was the remainder of $9,000. But I wasn't going to give him the satisfaction of leaving, even though we were playing 3-handed (which is an intense situation under normal circumstances). Mind you, he still cared about me, despite not wanting to live with me any longer.

He anted; I anted. My door card was a king; his was an ace. The low card brought it in to open the pot. I raised, and the LOML reraised. I turned to him and said, "Just show me the aces, and I'll pick up my chips and leave." He sat expressionless. I didn't know whether his reraise was a power play or if he really had aces, but I was determined that I wasn't going to be dumped and then bluffed on top of it. I put in the rest of my measly stack. After the dealer dealt the seventh card, the LOML turned over aces. That was the closest I ever came to crying at a poker table.

The moral of this story is that when you're playing cards,

even the person who loved you for seven years, if he's a pro, is unlikely to show you any compassion. So what do you think the person who's known you for seven minutes is feeling about your breakup?

TIP 16

Do not attempt to learn seven-card stud and Texas hold 'em simultaneously.

Texas hold 'em and seven-card stud look similar because they're both played with 52 cards, and the hierarchy of winning hands is the same. But the concepts for one game are quite different from those of the other, because hold 'em is a community card game whereas in stud each player receives an individual hand. (The specifics are outlined in Appendix 4.) I strongly recommend learning one game thoroughly (as long as a year's worth of study) before attempting to master the other. Trying to learn both simultaneously will create confusion and a crossover of concepts. The most likely result will be that you'll stink at both games. Following are a few reasons why you might prefer one game over the other, as well as some of the specific playing differences.

SEVEN-CARD STUD IS A CARD-READING GAME

Stud favors the alert, detective-type mind with a keen and methodical memory. Patience is highly rewarded. Because there are many open cards, it's very much like solving a mystery; each card revealed offers an additional clue. It is far more mentally exhausting to play stud than hold 'em because of the continual need to concentrate. Weaker players have a better chance of winning in stud, as the luck factor is bigger (which is frustrating because your fluctuations will be higher).

HOLD 'EM IS MORE OF A PEOPLE-READING GAME

Texas hold 'em is easily learned and deceptively simple. It suits the personality who likes fast, fast, fast, because there are fewer open cards and one less betting round. But if you're playing against experienced players and you lack aggression, you'll be an appetizer in a piranha tank. If you are adept at analyzing betting patterns, you'll be adept at gaining information, but if you're not, you'll be doing a lot of guesswork. If you are a bluffer, it's a far more effective tool in hold 'em than in stud.

> Generally, the stud aficionados believe their game is more difficult, and hold 'em players think the same.

There is debate among experts on which game requires more skill. My experience is that hold 'em is routine in a full game but highly complex short-handed. Stud is always a challenge, whether you're playing in a full game or short-handed, but your playing decisions at the river are not as difficult as hold 'em. Generally, the stud aficionados believe their game is more difficult, and hold 'em players think the same.

HOW THEY'RE DIFFERENT

Here are a few examples of why the playing concepts are different for each game:

1. High cards hold more value in hold 'em. A-K is a good starting hand in hold 'em, but A-K/3 offsuit is an abysmal hand in a full stud game.
2. The odds of making a **drawing hand*** differ, because stud has one more betting round. A flush draw can be a monster hand in stud on fourth street, but not such a big hand in hold 'em on the **flop****.
3. Because the major portion of your hand is determined by the flop in hold 'em, stud players have a hard time resisting the impulse to continue attempting to catch a winning card with only two more cards to come.
4. Hold 'em players often are drawing dead on sixth street in stud, because they are ignorant of the value of pairs versus high cards.
5. Stud players waste too much money calling bets unnecessarily on the river in hold 'em. In contrast, hold 'em players are too easily bluffed on the river in stud.

Players who understand both games usually find they are stronger in the one they learned first. It is rare to find players who are equally competent in both.

*Drawing hand—**four cards to a straight or flush with more cards to come.**

Flop—in hold 'em-type games, the first three cards turned faceup after the first betting round.**

TIP 17

Do not let a misguided ego interfere with your earn.

The ego is good when it provides us with a healthy sense of self-confidence, resilience, and strength. But it's bad when it causes us to make foolish choices that decrease our win rate. You might benefit from thinking you're the greatest if you actually *are* the greatest (like Muhammad Ali and Joe Namath), but if you're not, that lack of objectivity (a crucial aspect to poker) will be a quick way of depositing money from your bankroll directly into another's.

POKER REQUIRES A MULTIDIMENSIONAL PERSONALITY

A pitcher would never get to the major leagues if he could throw only a fastball, because he would be too predictable. The same is true of a poker player—if she could not make change-ups, every move would be anticipated by her opponent. Your ego must have the capacity to inflate and deflate rapidly as a means of deceiving your opponent.

Here's one scenario of how ego can send you offtrack: You've just graduated from $6/$12 to $15/$30, and hopefully you have said adios to the smaller limit forever. But what happens if you get unlucky at your new level and your bankroll dictates you drop back down and rebuild. Are you capable of doing so? Or do you fear the veiled remarks from your buds who were secretly hoping you'd fail so they could feel better about themselves? It's more dignified to step down now then go broke later.

Here's another scenario: What if suddenly you look around the table and there isn't one player who plays worse than you? In fact, there are many players who are better. But you're stuck, there's no other table open, and you don't want your opponents to smirk as you sidle into the shadows. I hear your ego rationalizing, if I get up now, it'll be a concession that I'm not as good as them. I'll look scared. Your ego is trying to trip you up. Unless there is a strong possibility that the game dynamics will change quickly, get your fanny out of the chair and either play lower or go home and play hide-and-seek with the cat. Don't be a victim of your own ego; you win only when other players make mistakes. If they aren't likely to, you're wasting your time.

You win only when other players make mistakes. If they aren't likely to, you're wasting your time.

Scenario No. 3: You have been waiting for ages to sit in a game with a major fish. A seat opens. But oops, the fish packs up and swims away, and now the other players begin to leave the game. Yikes! Within minutes you find yourself playing four-handed, and your tension grows with each new deal; you don't have the experience or the bankroll for short-handed fluctuations. It is true that if you get up immediately, the players left will be mildly amused or even say something to embarrass you, but who gives a big hootie! No one will be thinking about you 10 seconds after your exit. Don't let a prideful ego dictate your decisions because you want to appear as someone you're not.

Scenario No. 4: Dick doesn't like you because you've been **holding over*** him and you don't like him because he's an oinker. He's miffed and wants to prove once and for all who is the best poker player, you or him, and he makes a public challenge to a **heads-up**** match. He'll try to manipulate you into saying yes by forcing you to concede that he's better if you refuse the challenge. In actuality your skills are very close, and it would only be a matter of who was dealt the luckiest cards.

The practical reason to decline is that you won't make as much money playing Dick as you will staying put in the game you're presently playing. The emotional reason to decline is that there is never a more personal and painful loss than losing to someone whom you dislike. So tell him, "No thanks." You may have to grin and bear it when he says, "You're just a mediocre scared girl on a short run of good luck." I could offer you some pithy comebacks, but if you used them, it would make your mother wonder how she raised you. So let's settle on, "I play heads-up only with members of the human race," or "I don't need to play heads-up to know who the champion is." Don't let your ego goad you into playing a match you might not regret just today, but for months to come.

> "Big egos and big losses go hand in hand."
>
> —John Gollehon
> *A Gambler's Little Instruction Book*

Which gender is more susceptible to the failing of having to prove "I'm better than you"? Don't be so fast to pin it on the one who originated the pissing matches because, honestly, both sexes are vulnerable.

***Holding over*—means you consistently have been dealt better cards than another player.**

****Heads-up*—involving a game with only two players.**

At one time or another, we all become obsessed with what someone thinks about us. In truth, people are so self-absorbed that they're really not spending that much time thinking about us at all. If you need your ego massaged, visit your best friend; don't go to the poker room.

TIP 18

Do not play if your hormones are carrying hand grenades.

Some women feel like Farrah Fawcett in the '70s during their premenstrual periods, and believe me, I wish I were one of them. But there are those of us who suffer under the influence of intoxicating hormones. If you're one of these unlucky ones, I have some advice for you. Playing poker is a unique pursuit, because it always strikes the heart of your emotional core. You literally cannot afford to play if you're experiencing *any* of the following symptoms: mood swings, anger, anxiety, lack-of-concentration, tearfulness, or lowered self-esteem. I am not limited to one or two of these symptoms; I go for a circus act of juggling at least four or five, and although I can astonish a crowd, no one has yet to applaud. For years I didn't acknowledge that

I was too impaired to play poker while experiencing PMS, because I was too stupid or too stubborn to keep track on the calendar. The proof, however, was in my wallet—which was the only thing on me that wasn't getting bloated!

There was one irritable monthly incident that could have cost me a fortune. An obnoxious player had taken $90,000 worth of chips and put them in a flimsy plastic bag. There was a tray table between us, and each time I stopped to concentrate he'd smack the bag against the wood, and its loud crack completely splintered my focus. I said to him, "Do that once more and you'll be sorry." *Smack! Crack!* I grabbed the bag from him and threw it over my head. It sailed over the railing that separates the high-limit games from the low-limit ones, and the bag split. Ninety thousand dollars worth of chips scattered everywhere—in the middle of one ongoing pot, in players' stacks, on the floor, even in somebody's wonton soup. Needless to say, there was a lot of movement as fingers started grabbing and pocketing the chips, and no one was moving faster than yours truly as I pleaded with the security guards to help me pick them up.

> "Women complain about PMS, but I think it's the only time of the month I can be myself."
>
> —Rosanne Barr

I contend that you can play poker during PMS if you get **hit with the deck***, but it takes only one ordinary event, such as flopping **set under set****, or your nemesis showing a bluff, and the period ogre will emerge. Suddenly your betting hand will disconnect from your brain, and you'll be

***Hit with the deck—being dealt an unusual number of good cards.**

****Set under set—in hold 'em when two people both flop trips; also referred to as "set over set."**

reraising like its Monopoly money. So humor me: Just keep track in your record books of those few vulnerable days before your period and see if there is any pattern of financial dips. If there is, give yourself a vacation from poker until the clouds disappear and your serotonin levels normalize. For that act of discipline and honesty, I will applaud you.

TIP 19

Do not play poker under the influence of alcohol, mind-altering drugs, or pain medication.

"Duh," I can hear you saying. "Who doesn't know that?" Well, there's a difference between knowing and actually adhering to the advice. We've all got to make our own mistakes, but I hope at least a handful of you can avoid an embarrassing loss by hearing about some of mine.

TEQUILA POKER AT CAESAR'S PALACE

In the days before I played poker as a profession, I played for the stimulation of action and to mix it up socially after a blackjack session. I had a bad-influence friend (lots of fun with lots of addictions), and one evening he suggested that we add a twist to the game: Whoever won a hand had to drink a shot of tequila. The game turned into a party, and seven out of the eight players at our table joined our idiocy. After the fifth shot, I was trying to make a flush and accidentally backed into a straight, which I failed to notice because I was tipsy. I turned my hand faceup in disgust (looking for sympathy I wasn't going to get), then scooped up my cards and quickly mucked them. That's when the dealer said, "Ma'am, did you realize you made a straight?" Losing $800 was almost as bad as being called "ma'am," but the $800 error probably did more to sober me up. The game ended when my friend tipped over backward out of his chair and management asked us to leave.

> "Never mix cards and whiskey unless you were weaned on Irish poteen."
>
> —Margaret Mitchell
> *Gone with the Wind*

It shouldn't be too hard to guess who won all the cash in tequila poker—the designated driver. Even if your session is almost over and you want to unwind in the game with a glass of wine, don't do it until the counting is done. You never know when a fish might show up in a tuxedo and change the exit plan.

THE MARY-JANE POKER GAME

In the days when hippies were cooler than yuppies, I went outside with my friend to listen to a bad-beat story. He relit a roach and extended the doobie to me. I thought it would be kind of fun to play stoned, so I inhaled like he was doing me a favor. When I got back to the game, all I kept thinking was, please, Goddess of Cards, don't give me a hand—I just want to watch, because things that never interested me before, like Arnie's twitching mustache when he's bluffing, are so damn fascinating. I got stuck with the **bring-in*** and tried to memorize the cards out—yup, two nines and two sevens were on the board. Within seconds (or it could have been minutes, who knows, I was stoned), my memory reversed the dead cards on the board with my hole cards. When I caught a nine on fourth street, I thought I'd made a pair; when I caught a seven on fifth street, I thought I'd made two pair. On sixth street my opponent bet, and I raised him with my imaginary two pair. After I bet the river and my opponent called, I triumphantly turned over my hand and announced, "Two pair." My opponent did a double take and said, "Honey, get it fixed. You think you're playing with kids?"

I still think it was a bad beat that I managed to catch the two cards that I'd memorized on the board, but I'm going to be hard-pressed to get any sympathy from anyone but a druggie. Marijuana, in particular, although it assists in patience, gives you the short-term memory of a flea. If you have a money tree in your backyard, keep on toking Sister Sunshine.

THE GAME WITH NO PAIN

Before I joined the "Just Say No!" campaign, I stopped in the poker room after having a root canal at the dentist's office. My tooth was throbbing, so I popped a pain killer. It was heaven playing, because anytime I lost I didn't feel a twinge of sorrow or remorse. I was brain-numb, and I just kept on losing and giggling. I wasn't necessarily playing poorly, but I wasn't giving a thought to stopping, because it was so enjoyable to play

*Bring-in—**the amount required to open the pot.**

without experiencing the pain of losing. It's important, though, that you feel the pain when you start losing, even if it's only to be aware of your table image. Everyone at the table took note of my downward spiral and started chasing and eventually outplaying me. Believe me, when the Percocet wore off, I felt plenty. Moral of this story: A little pain can prevent an unnatural disaster.

TIP 20

Give it all you've got, regardless of your friendly relationship with an opponent.

Have you ever watched a bang-up NBA game between two stars and thought they were each other's worst enemy? Yet after the game they give each other a sweat-drenched hug? If you're a woman, it can be confusing. How can you put an elbow in someone's jaw in the third quarter and 12 minutes later make plans to meet for a beer?

The women players I know are reluctant to play their hardest against a friend who is on the down-and-out. Men, on the other hand, can play tough against each other at the table and not be dizzied out by a sneaky check-raise. A man doesn't care if his pal's wife is going to leave him if he comes home broke. If his friend's got $20 left, he's going to try and win it. It's all part of the game.

I have a very dear girlfriend who suffered the misfortune of being in a near-death car accident. She broke at least 10 bones in various parts of her body, and wheeled herself up to the poker table with casts on her leg and arm. She's one tough Oklahoma girl, because if I were her, I'd have been catching up on the last 20 years of *General Hospital.* I was positioned on her left with buried kings. I didn't want her to become involved with an inferior hand, because she could be tricked by the strength of mine. I just turned my kings faceup. She turned up her hand, and she had buried aces and was, of course, a big favorite to win a healthy-sized pot. My acting like a girly-girl robbed her of a money-making advantage. She calmly said, "Don't ever do that again. We're competitors first at the poker table."

> "When I play with you for a sum I tell you in effect I'll do my best to spoil your diversion, to send you home with your head disturb'd, your pocket light and your heart heavy."
>
> —Jeremy Collier
> "An Essay on Gaming in a Dialogue between Callimachus and Dolomedes"

Here's another example that, if you're a woman, may make you cringe. If you're a man, you'll probably think: Hey, it's poker. What did you expect? My best friend was on a losing streak that had turned his brain into Cream of Wheat and his heart into Silly Putty. He lost a tough hand, and I could see he was shook-up. I suggested that we take a break from our game so I could give him a pep talk. Outside I rallied around him like a Lakers cheerleader: Siss!—you're the best—Boom!—you're the greatest—Bah!—you're a champ, blah-ti-dah! When we went back inside, the first hand he played was against me. Ordinarily I wouldn't fold a pair of aces on sixth street, but I never thought he'd have the audacity to bluff me after my pom-pom oratory. He showed me the bluff after I folded, and it was six years before I pulled the pins out of the voodoo doll and released him from my double-whammy hex.

As you can see, this is one of those do-as-I-say-and-not-as-I-do tips. If you're even remotely a softy, avoid playing against a good friend because it may jeopardize the friendship. But if you're more mature, play hard and just be ready to buy the beer.

4

Be All You Can Be Without Joining the Army

Basic Boot Camp Advice

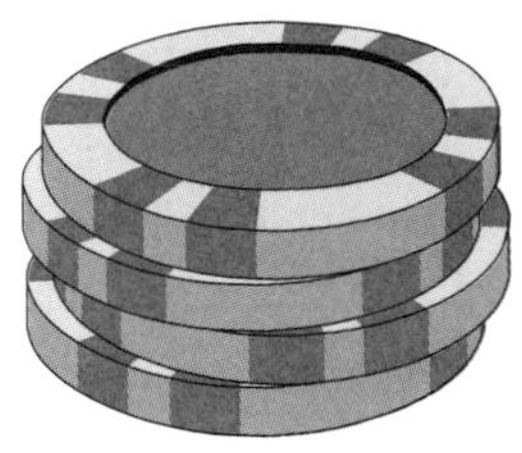

TIP 21

Begin your session calm.

Imagine yourself in an extravagant fantasy: You're on the sands of a white beach in Maui with nothing to do for six days but read, swim, and flirt with the cabana boy. The seventh day would be the ideal time to begin a poker session. Your body would be relaxed from your Saturday-night date with the lifeguard; your mind would be free from worries, fresh and entirely in the moment.

On the flip side, imagine that you've just gone to a Lakers playoff game, screamed your lungs hoarse, bet on the wrong side, and upon exiting discovered that you'd forgotten where you parked, causing you to hike around a bad neighborhood for an hour in shoes that pinch. Your mind is jazzed up, you don't feel tired and you want to get back that $100 you lost on the game. There's a casino just a short detour off your route home. It's midnight, but it shouldn't take you more than an hour to make that money back. (I know who is going to wish she'd brought her sunglasses when the sun comes up.)

> "He had the calm confidence of a Christian with four aces."
>
> —Mark Twain

I used sledge-hammer examples for a reason: I want you to immediately recognize the advantage of starting a session with an unfettered brain. Poker is a game best suited to a calm mind, because it requires deep concentration and the ability to make well thought-out decisions very quickly. It's obvious the quiet brain is more apt to make the right choices, remain objective about a losing hand, not let any offhand remarks get under your skin, and learn from any errors you may make.

If you are a full-time player, construct your day to have minimal activity before going to your "job." If you're a part-time player who is interested in improving her game and making money, don't sit down at the table after a grueling day as an emergency-room nurse. Play on your days off, or take a yoga class after work that will help relax your head and body. If you're a napper, enjoy some zzzzzzzzs before you play. Even if you simply consider yourself a "desperate housewife" who plays to get together with her friends to laugh and gossip about Wisteria Lane, remind yourself that this is *your* time, tuck your errand list away, turn off your cell phone, and focus on the game.

If you're a napper, enjoy some zzzzzzzzs before you play.

Good grief, you may be thinking, this author doesn't want me to walk and chew gum at the same time. Not so. This author simply wants you to sit down to play with a clear and focused brain, and there isn't a professional player who would disagree with me. Poker requires a calm internal and external state for you to be a winner.

TIP 22

Do not box yourself in by a set quitting time.

Poker and punching a time clock are not compatible. It's best not to make a post-poker commitment, because you'll either break it or feel constrained by the limitations. I'm a horrible offender of this rule and have the reputation for flaking out on obligations. For me, there isn't an activity (including eating dinner) that's as enjoyable or engrossing as poker.

Even if you're not obsessed with poker, there are logical reasons not to box yourself into a quitting time. First, if you're winning like Porky Pig, it's an opportune time to take advantage of a strong image and win even more. Those times don't occur often, and it's a shame if you have to leave because you have a four o'clock hair appointment. Second, the game itself may be so ripe for profit that if you have to leave, you'll think you're costing yourself money (and you will be). You'll be resentful of whatever task or person is responsible for your departure. Third, when you are losing and you have your eye on the clock, many hands you wouldn't ordinarily play begin to look juicy because you feel the urgency to get even. That's a weakness that most pros have, although we know it's irrational.

> "You can't gamble by the clock . . . Time can place a limitation on pleasure."
>
> —Nick "The Greek" Dandalos

To demonstrate the unreliability of poker players, I'll relate a short story about my 40th birthday party. I threw a catered soiree with a live five-piece rock band. I invited 60 people from the poker room to celebrate with me. Fifty players said, "Absolutely, can't wait. I'll be there." At 8 P.M. the 10 people who had come sat embarrassed with me in my backyard, as I coaxed them to make their third trip to the buffet table in the hopes of seeing at least a dent in the two-story mound of potato salad. I didn't hold a grudge against the no-shows; I've done it myself. I was late for my sister's wedding when I was the maid of honor, and I skipped Thanksgiving when I was supposed to bring the turkey.

But instead of letting someone down by the tired-out excuse, "Stuck in a poker game" (which only poker players accept as valid), avoid setting a fixed quitting time unless you are optionless. Whether you're winning or losing, the skill level of players in the game, your attitude and mental clarity, and your physical stamina should be the determining factors for leaving the game, not your Timex.

Set Your Priorities

If you know you're the type to get sucked into a game and flake out on commitments, here's an obvious suggestion: Don't play on days when you really have to be somewhere else. Being respected as a reliable person is an important character trait. If you told Aunt Sally that you'd visit her in the hospital in the evening, don't go to the casino until after you see her. Being dependable is far more important than winning the next hand. Aunt Sally might not be around forever, but poker will be.

TIP 23

Sit as far away as you can from expert players at the poker table.

When you're choosing your seat, try to position yourself between weak players rather than between strong ones. The reason is that you'll be playing more pots with the opponents to your left and right. This is because of the battle of the blinds in hold 'em and the fight for the antes in stud. A neighbor player raising after all the other players have folded is far more likely to be on a **steal*** than an early position raiser who knows he still has to contend with several players. It's just like when your bicycle is missing—you don't worry about someone from Mozambique being the thief, but you might look over the picket fence and see whether one of the neighborhood kids is the culprit.

You have to take a stand against an overly aggressive neighbor, because he's the one most likely to rip you off.

You have to take a stand against an overly aggressive neighbor, because he's the one most likely to rip you off. If he identifies you as a meek pushover, he's going to run all over

***Steal—to win a pot by bluffing.**

you like syrup on a pancake. At some point, whether you have a premium hand or have to pick him off by bluffing, you're going to have to slow down his larceny by reraising.

CULTIVATE YOUR NEIGHBORS

If you have a neighbor who blasts Snoop Dogg at midnight, which course of action do you think would be most effective in getting a good night's sleep—calling the police or inviting him to your next barbecue? It's the same in poker. Build a positive relationship with Mr. Right and Mr. Left. Use their first names, ask about the kids, and show an interest in them as people. If you're a woman, this is as easy as spending $50 at the cosmetics counter. If the player on your right likes you, he's less likely to rob you; if the player on your left likes you, he's more apt to believe your steal is a legitimate hand.

> "The Bible tells us to love our neighbors, and also to love our enemies; probably because generally they are the same people."
>
> —Gilbert K. Chesterton

If the players on your right and left are true experts, they won't be slowed down by an occasional reraise because they can smell intimidation like wolves in a sheep pen. Experts understand that aggression is a powerful weapon in capturing the feeder monies and are willing to take more risks than average players. Constantly capturing the blinds and antes with a raise, when no one has a legitimate playing hand, adds up to an easy stream of uncontested profit. Don't try to outplay this type; instead take a seat where you can wear the wolf's clothing.

TIP 24

Mentally focus on your strengths—it'll help you exude a winning image.

Creating an image of authority at the poker table comes naturally from the soul and it's an issue of self-esteem. The better you feel about yourself, the greater the chance that you will become the force to reckon with.

Many aspects of society undermine a woman's confidence: the overemphasis on beauty, the paltry number of female versus male senators in the United States Senate*, the percentage of women CEOs in *Forbes* 500, and women adopting their husbands' surnames, not to mention the mundane aspects of life that are viewed as a woman's domain and less important than earning a living—like changing diapers, housework, buying groceries, etcetera. All of this often translates into a woman believing she has to fight for equal rights rather than equality being her natural birthright. Men aren't totally responsible for our struggle; in many ways we bring it on ourselves by fostering feelings of mental and physical inadequacies. Why do we spend the time on inner disapproval when it causes us to stumble at every challenge?

***In 2005 there were fourteen female senators in the U.S. Senate and eighty-six male senators.**

When a woman sits at a poker table and thinks men are the more important gender, she gives them the power to beat her. If you are a woman who feels this way, you are going to have to compensate in other ways to project an authoritative image. Don't ever think bad thoughts about yourself or put yourself down. If it takes reading 202 self-help books on the subject of undoing an inferiority complex, read them. If you didn't grow up with the word "proud" in your vocabulary, add it now. Even if you have to listen to Helen Reddy roar 30 times "I Am Woman" to psych yourself up before you sit down at a poker table, do it. Do whatever it takes; don't accept being second-best as the natural order. If there is a negative influence in your life, like a mother or a husband, who makes you feel as valuable as leftover meatloaf, you may need therapeutic help to neutralize that person's power. But take some kind of action to be the only one painting your self-portrait.

Even if you have to listen to Helen Reddy roar 30 times "I Am Woman" to psych yourself up before you sit down at a poker table, do it.

DON'T BRING YOUR INSECURITIES TO THE POKER TABLE

When you're about to play poker, go over the list in your mind of things you excel at; think about the last time you got an A, the last compliment you received. Evoke memories that make you smile—the spelling bee you won in third grade for spelling logarithm (without knowing what it meant). Remember the times you shared a piece of yourself and felt appreciated, the precious moment when a friend said, "I won't bet you; you're always right." Engage in pre-poker activities that promote a positive self-image, such as making your kids laugh, finishing a project, or changing the oil in your husband's car. When you're self-confident, you have more energy, think more clearly, and—most important—feel happier and have a greater chance for success at poker or at anything else you do.

Here's your poker mantra: I'm strong enough, I'm smart enough, and—gosh darn it—I *will* win your money.

I believe our time is up for this tip. That'll be $185, please, and I'll see you next session.

TIP 25

Remember that poker requires extreme patience and self-control.

Test your patience quotient:

1. Do the words "Please hold" make you wish Alexander Graham Bell had never been born?
2. Have you ever been known to read mystery novels backward just to have the satisfaction of thinking, I know who done it?

3. Are you liable to make tubercular cough noises in line at Rite Aid hoping someone in front of you will get the willies and let you jump the line?
4. Does your greyhound hide when it's time for a walk because it's just too brisk outside?
5. Do you wish your boyfriend would forget about foreplay?
6. Is your Lean Cuisine half-frozen because the microwave wasn't quick enough?
7. Has an ambulance driver ever asked to follow you to the hospital because you're driving faster than him?
8. Does a New York minute feel like a half hour?

If you answered yes to more than two questions, we have some work to do. Poker has spurts of exhilaration, but a large percentage of the time you're at the table you won't be actively playing a hand. You may not even play one hand in 10, because the reality is that sometimes the card goddess simply withholds her bounty. Sometimes you'll sit for two hours, mucking, mucking, mucking, wondering if you'll ever get a break. When this happens, do not get envious of the player who raises six hands in a row—*eventually* the cards will even out, and he'll be twiddling his thumbs when you're at the controls. Suddenly—whippity wham—you'll look down and find a pair of queens at 1:30 P.M., aces at 1:37 P.M., and kings at 1:43 P.M. (But don't be dialing the psychic hotline to find out the exact time of "eventually." I don't want to disillusion you,

Do not get envious of the player who raises six hands in a row—*eventually* the cards will even out, and he'll be twiddling his thumbs when you're at the controls.

but the wait might be longer than it takes to lose two pounds.)

If you watch the World Poker Tour on TV, remember that the program has been edited to maintain heightened viewer interest. If you had to watch every hand that was dealt, you'd happily switch over to *Bowling for Dollars* for stimulation.

I have never thought poker as tedious or dull, but I have heard others say so. My advice is, if you find it boring to be disciplined and to wait for good starting hands, take up racquetball. If you are really doing your job, there are dozens of game-related observations to occupy your brain while you wait, and you should never lack for something to think about.

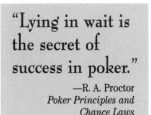

> "Lying in wait is the secret of success in poker."
>
> —R. A. Proctor
> *Poker Principles and Chance Laws*

Don't try to rationalize playing a mediocre hand because you're afraid the other players will think you're too **tight***. One of the great things about being a woman is that some dope can tell the table you're a **rock****, and the first time you raise in an hour you'll get four callers, plus the dope will stupidly reraise.

If you failed my Patience Quotient Quiz, take heart—20 years ago I talked so fast that even New Yorkers had a hard time understanding me. It was ingrained from my blackjack days: Fast was smart; slow was stupid. But if I could slow down and be more in the moment, you can too. Here are some ways to start: Read every word of a poem (then read it again), don't fast-forward the movie credits, stop interrupting, give up swearing, slow down as the light turns yellow, chew even the healthy bites slowly, offer the one-item shopper your spot

***Tight—when you're playing very conservatively.**
****Rock—a super-tight player.**

in the checkout line, actually wait until Christmas day to open your presents, sit down and write a newsy letter to your grandmother. Once you get the hang of it, you'll find dozens of ordinary ways to practice the art of being patient.

TIP 26

Create the illusion of gambling.

As a woman, it is not necessary to throw money away on advertising that you're a wild and crazy gambler to get action. A man may have said to himself 20 times, "That lady is so tight, if she bets I'm going to fold faster than a beer pitcher is chugged at a frat party." But when the time comes to heed his own counsel, he can't help himself—it's back to, "What could she have?" It's often true for both men and women that you don't have to give action to get action.

Still, not all men are chumps, and a few are worldly enough to realize that women can be very good players. For them there's a secret trick, a magic illusion that you should perform when the time is right. Bet when you know you'd call if your opponent bet. Think about that. For example, in stud, your board on fifth street develops into 9-10-J (you have a queen in the pocket), and your opponent raised with a 10 showing on third street. He's going to be afraid that you may have outdrawn him. He won't be willing to fold, but he won't be raising you either because you have a three-straight on your board, as well as an **overcard*** to his 10.

> "Take calculated risks. That is quite different from being rash."
>
> —General George S. Patton

There are other even-money situations (approximately) in which you can become the aggressor in stud and raise your opponent on a strong drawing hand, such as a four-flush with an overcard to his door card. This works well in hold 'em when you raise on the flop in last position and take a **free card**** on the turn (fourth upcard) if you don't complete your hand. Aggressive plays like the ones just described are perceived as gambling, but you are simply taking control of the hand in very close situations.

I also like the play of occasionally raising with marginal hands on the river for extra value in stud. For instance, you think your opponent has one high pair and you've made two pair. Raise him occasionally. You may make an extra bet, get him to fold the best hand, or definitely get him to back off from betting one pair into you at the river.

Watch for other opponents who are savvy enough to make similar plays and record them in your player's notebook. Such plays are a tell-tale sign of a good player who knows where the magician hides the rabbit.

*Overcard—**in stud, a card in your hand higher than any card showing among your opponents' exposed cards. In hold 'em, a card in a player's hand that is of higher rank than the exposed community cards.**

Free card—the situation where there is no bet on a particular round.**

5

Only Your Hairdresser (and Shrink) Knows for Sure

The Importance of Maintaining Your Privacy

TIP 27

Gain information about others, but zip your lips about yourself.

Like a woman behind a feather mask at a costume ball, you want to keep the intrigued strangers at the poker table guessing about your identity. Anonymous doesn't mean invisible; it can be maddeningly mysterious to leave your opponents in a state of curiosity. Knowing exactly who you are enables them to play better poker against you, especially if you spill the beans on your experience level.

The pros will attempt to extract pertinent information. I know, I'm the Jane Pauley of green-felt interviews. If I can extract simple facts that appear innocent—your profession, what type of car you drive, how often you vacation, what neighborhood you live in—I can gain clues as to the size of your bankroll. Suppose, for instance, my opponent just mentioned that his yacht was rented for an episode of *Will & Grace*. I can assume he's got *beaucoup* bucks and I imagine that he'll be more willing to splash around with imaginative starting hands and to risk bluffing. He may be competitive as hell, but his motivation for playing poker is entertainment. Even a simple statement, such as, "I usually play the small games, but today I'm taking a shot at playing higher," is revealing. It shows that the player could be experiencing some discomfort about the stakes and probably will be playing close to the cuff.

My eyes are wide open even in the parking lot. I want to know who rides together and who takes pains to avoid each other. If an unlikely pair is sharing a toke at the far end of the lot, I want to take note. Likewise, if two players sit down in the same game acting as if they don't know each other, but I saw them chatting at the entrance, it's definitely a situation that makes me go "hmmm."

If two players sit down in the same game acting as if they don't know each other, but I saw them chatting at the entrance, it's definitely a situation that makes me go "hmmm."

I also make it a point to be poker-room aware. I glance around to see whom I've played with before (and hopefully recall their usual limits, game preferences, how often they play). I take particular note of anything unusual. If Tammy has played low-limit stud for two years and suddenly appears at my high-limit hold 'em table, I'll bet there's something other than poker on her mind. If Gandhoff has always played high-limit poker and now is playing two levels below, I can assume he's been on a losing streak. Likewise, if the rumor is that Nathan just got out of jail for stealing his girlfriend's car, I'm going to be watching him very carefully when his hands go anywhere near the pot.

Plus the shoulder strap of my purse will be attached to my ankle. Also, if Nathan is best buddies with Charlie, what does that say about Charlie? Friends with similar ethics tend to cluster together in the poker room, as in life. Good guys hang with good guys, and bad guys hang with bad.

The better you are at subtly gleaning odds and ends about a player's life, the better poker you will play against him. But this works both ways, so don't be too trusting when the pro asks something innocent like, "Are you married?" If you are, the pro understands there's a better chance you have a curfew. If you're a total banana brain and even give him the time you have to be home, he'll know as the zero hour approaches that if you're stuck, you're likely to open up your game, and if you're trying to lock up a win, you'll probably play more conservatively.

You want to be congenial but not give away any ammunition. Beware of seemingly innocent questions like where you went to college and what was your major. If you're an MIT grad with a math major, I'm going to be a lot more worried than if you went to Cobleskill Agricultural College. A math major is surely more likely to know the odds of when she should pay off a bet because she's getting the right price. On the other hand, you never know whether that aggie will turn out to have a more beautiful mind than John Nash! Which brings me to my next point: Don't fall too far into the trap of stereotyping. Remember, others may value privacy just as much as you do.

Beware of seemingly innocent questions like where you went to college and what was your major.

The more personal the information you share, the worse the mistake. All sensitive issues can be used as weapons by an antagonistic foe. I once revealed that I was facing a quality-of-life decision about my beloved Akitas. On another day, a player who had overheard that discussion gleefully told premature euthanasia pet stories, absolutely certain I would become unraveled. He was right, but I was smart enough to end my session. I consider that player evil, but the reality is that I can't blame anyone but myself. Some mistakes you learn the hard way.

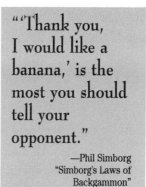

> "'Thank you, I would like a banana,' is the most you should tell your opponent."
>
> —Phil Simborg
> "Simborg's Laws of Backgammon"

Be equally suspicious of everyone—even the nice guys, the good-looking stud, and that sweet nerd who's kindly inquiring if you have any little ones at home. Know that being the lady in red will be more beneficial to your game and more fun than being the 47-year-old going through her second divorce and waiting on her alimony check from old Deadbeat Dad.

If someone is insistently digging for information, you have a few alternatives. Lying is acceptable when it's truly none of his business. If you're imaginative, make up a whopper. Men are jealous of women who were born lucky; tell him your grandmother just left you a million-dollar inheritance. Add that you play poker to supplement your income to pay for your live-in chef. My mentor, who is nicknamed "The Gentleman," always made me giggle when someone asked him where he lived in L.A. He'd dryly reply, "Cudahy," a section of the city where even gangbangers are afraid to cruise at night. If you want to make a player back off, the best two answers you can give are: 1) you work for the Internal Revenue Service or 2) you just got transferred to the NYPD narcotics unit.

A coy woman with a secret agenda might even say, "Ask my bodyguard." Other ploys you can try include mumbling until he gives up trying to hear you, speaking in an indecipherable foreign language, just laughing, or signing in ASL, "Darling, I just want to be left alone." If dissembling isn't your bag, try bluntness. Saying, "Give me a break; I need to concentrate" will send a clear-cut message.

Eventually, men will either give up trying to cross the fortress drawbridge or get drowned in the crocodile-infested moat. But initially, you're the one who has to build your castle out of stone. Even one breach of security can cause a leak of information that floods the poker room with gossip. Because it's a fact, men like to ignite rumor as much as anyone.

TIP 28

Do not try to change the world at the poker table.

Among players of most competitive sports and games, there is a certain amount of trash talk and shtick. (I've heard that even the saintly Michael Jordan had a reputation for talking bullshit to rattle his opponents during a game.) The poker table can be like an NBA game without referees, and sometimes your virgin ears will hear things that shock, offend, and turn them as red as a stop

What to Do When You Just Have to Do Something

When someone is acting like a major jerk, instead of losing your cool or having a self-righteous hissy fit, try these alternative measures for righting a wrong:

You can take the dealer aside when he's on a break and explain that we're all not like that schmo who acted like such a putz. Another route is to do a random act of kindess for a stranger to counteract the karma, or take a break and try to shed the icky feeling, or alert the floorperson if a dealer is being abused, or, best of all, all three.

sign. There's one opponent in my regular game whose nickname is "Muthafucker," which suits him because it's the only word I've ever heard him utter.

You might also see players treat ordinary hard-working people—like the waiter or the dealer—in ways that will make your blood boil. A self-important owner of a Jiffy Lube franchise once got a porter fired for calling him "Buddy." He demanded to be called "Sir" by his inferiors. Yes, he did use the word "inferiors." Later when he called me "Cat," I spoke up and told him, "I insist you address me only as 'Catherine Jeanine,' or even better, don't speak to me at all." Ignorant players will blame the dealer after losing a hand and will intentionally try to clip the dealer's face or hands when pitching the cards into the discard pile.

How should you handle abuse that is directed at innocents? My poker teacher warned me never to interfere and to let it bounce off me instead of hiring on as a defense attorney. But my nature is to stick my big snout right in the middle of the foray, especially if I believe someone is being mistreated as a victim of prejudice.

I protested to my teacher: "But it's everyone's duty to stop ugly slurs and basic unkindness to other humans. How else can we change the world but to become involved? Letting bad behavior go is similar to watching a crime with detached interest!" My teacher's simple, but effective, response was, "How does it affect your poker?"

The truth is, whenever I got frazzled by the obnoxiousness of humankind, everywhere I looked I saw red. I was so blinded, I couldn't tell the difference between clubs and diamonds. I wanted to punish the perpetrator, whoever he was, so badly that I would have reraised him with **7-2 offsuit***. But whenever this happened, there were six other players at the table sitting back amused at the confrontation, waiting patiently for direct deposits into their bank accounts.

When my teacher reminded me that there are ways to settle human-rights disputes other than to froth at the mouth, it was a major turning point for me. I wasn't necessarily making the situation better with my interference, and sometimes the dealer (or whoever) actually preferred that I stay out of it. "If someone is a racist," my teacher inquired, "what chance do you think you have of changing his attitude by publicly embarrassing him?" But I protested, "If you can get the nitwit to keep his mouth shut in the future, it could demonstrate that some of us do not accept ignorance as an excuse." My teacher and I delved further into my rationale and my need to correct wrongs. He didn't think my motivation was anything

***7-2 offsuit—supposedly the worst starting hand in hold 'em, it has very little chance of becoming a winning hand because it doesn't contain high cards, nor does it have straight or flush potential.**

other than self-righteous indignation, which was hurtful, but I was willing to accept that the poker table is not the proper venue for changing the world.

There's always a time and a place for changing the world. But at the poker table, the cost of distraction, even when you've got right on your side, is going to be very expensive.

TIP 29

Do not engage in conversations that require an emotional investment.

Let's pretend you're a gay high-school Spanish teacher. Don't participate in conversations at the poker table that deal with bilingual education, gay rights, gay parents, gays in the military, home schooling, year-round schooling, teachers' salaries, hate crimes, or school violence. Any conversation that requires an emotional investment will entangle clarity with emotionalism, and you'll be thrown off your game. If any of those topics makes your hair stand on end, keep your mouth shut even if the Vietnam vet in seat No. 2 just said all gays are wimps and are not equipped to go to war. If you find a particular conversation so disturbing that your gut is busting to offer a counterpoint, take a break from the game.

That said, let's say the player to your right is a born-again Internet minister who believes in creationism, and he's been forcing his opinions down the throats of the players. In this case, do participate in already-started conversations on evolution, cloning, pro-choice versus pro-life, stem-cell research, assisted suicide, pornography, and sexual abuse by priests. In my book, initiating a conversation that you know will be upsetting to a particular opponent is underhanded, but participating in one he started is fair game. And let me point out the obvious: If it distracts you from your game, what in hell are you doing?

Take care to avoid revealing your personal politics and hot spots. Conversations outside of the realm of the ongoing game occur constantly at the poker table. You may long to disprove a theory that Joe Blowhard is spewing about the Maori people, but if it's one of your issues, close your mouth and resist talking about your last trip to New Zealand. As soon as you proffer an opinion, some player will think, ah ha, she has a soft spot for Australian Aborigines too, and you've given him a way to distract you a week from now. Conversations that decrease his comfort level, not yours, are the most profitable. Anyone care to discuss male sterilization?

Keep Your Cool

You're going to hear your share of chauvinistic quips, jokes, and barbs—all aimed at ruffling your composure. It's a male advantage if they can turn you into a woman who has an issue that needs defending. We aren't at the table to prove the superiority of the sexes. Remember, feminists can be as easily manipulated as chauvinists.

TIP 30

Never tell a player your home address!

I'll say it again: ***Never* tell a player your home address!**

Don't make me have to scare you by forcing you to watch multiple *Law & Order: Special Victims Unit* episodes with your eyelids glued open. We are women. We are vulnerable targets, especially when money is involved.

If you're the type who believes nothing bad can ever happen to you, I'll send you the police reports from the five times I was robbed (twice at gunpoint). Try to ignore that, Missy. Enough said? I hope so.

6

Anything He Can Do, She Can Do Better! (Except Lift a Piano)

Understanding the Strengths and Weaknesses of Being a Female Poker Player

TIP 31

Figure out your male opponents' attitudes toward women, and adjust your play accordingly.

Sexist attitudes are rampant at the poker table. This may not be pleasant, but it works to your advantage. The majority of men perceive a woman as incapable of intense competition. You will have to become more aggressive to survive, but you also can rely on the advantages of feminine cunning to keep your opponents distracted and off balance.

CHAUVINISM WEARS MANY DISGUISES

The Neanderthal chauvinist wants to force a woman into submission by conquering her sexually. If sex is not available to him, beating her pants off at the poker table will be a satisfying alternative. A Stone Age man would be so out of touch with the behavior of a twenty-first century woman that he wouldn't be any threat at the poker table. He'd have as much success figuring out what a modern woman is thinking as he would hunting for woolly mammoths on the Las Vegas Strip.

> "All men at the table will think about having sex with you. And there is only one out of 500 women they'd pass on, and only because she's 7 feet tall and needs a shave."
>
> —A $1,500/$3,000-Limit Bellagio Pro

Notice that the Bellagio pro said all men will want to have sex with you (see box). Can that be true? Obviously gay men won't, but a large majority of both gay and straight men agree that sex occupies as much as 60 percent of their thoughts. *All* men who are heterosexual will evaluate a woman's attractiveness when she sits down, and if she is attractive, they will fantasize about spending an hour in a cheap hotel. (Less than 30 minutes if they're losing.) However long the "sizing" takes, just your initial appearance is a distraction from the fundamental objective of poker.

MACHO, MACHO, MACHO MAN—I WISH THEY WERE ALL MACHO MEN

Poker has been a male-dominated arena for a long time, so how can we expect men to suddenly accept the presence of perfume and pheromones without grumbling? With the advent of women playing poker, men lose the freedom to curse and fart, and are suddenly faced with new rules of etiquette. The particularly gassy and foul-mouthed guys are going to be resentful. But no one will be more resentful than the macho man who can't stand to give up control or lose to anyone—especially to the opposite sex who should be home picking up his dirty underwear and chilling his Budweiser. Women are a particular threat to the machos, because disrupting their stereotype is similar to committing a perverse crime against man. At the poker table, women are aggressive aberrations and should be stamped out before we become a plague against the male-dominated world. How do you recognize the type? They smirk instead of smile, they talk to you without looking at you, and they have an arrogant posture.

> If he encounters a woman he can't intimidate, who feels no fear and is smart and articulate, his insecurities turn into rage.

My belief is that a macho man struggles with subconscious issues of cowardice and feeling stupid. If he encounters a woman he can't intimidate, who feels no fear and is smart and articulate, his insecurities turn into rage. He will overplay second-best and underplay the best, because he's bursting out of his Levi's to put you in your place. He doesn't just want to beat you; he wants to humiliate you.

Machos are a species to be laughed at, because it's so easy to manipulate their emotions and they usually aren't the best players at the table. In fact, they're often mediocre or just plain losers. If you win a hand against a macho, stack up his chips very slowly, extending the length of his anguish over losing. (If this seems mean, utilize the strategy only in deserved cases of revenge.) If you lose a hand, no matter how big a favorite you were, don't display any emotion. He wants to see you bleeding, but you're not a doe he's maimed in the woods because he's a bad shot. If he adds a verbal insult to the loss, muster a superior smile. Remain level-headed and you will win his chips. If you are faced with an iffy decision of whether to call on the river, call—because a man acting out of anger is more apt to make a desperate bluff. As far as bluffing him, he'll be so scared that you might show the bluff in front of the other men that he'll call with incredibly weak hands. So bluff cautiously, but always value-bet your medium-strength hands.

AND THE BAND KEEPS PLAYING "DADDY'S LITTLE GIRL"

Another psychologically interesting but transparent type of male opponent is "Daddykins." He'll want to show off to his little girl how much he knows about poker. This type of man longs for adoration. Listen, ask seemingly innocent questions, nod respectfully, never challenge an opinion, and mentally catalog everything he wants to share. The more a player divulges about how he thinks, the easier it is to develop a strategy to beat him. An added bonus is that Daddykins may be a good player and teach you some valuable tricks of the trade. He won't want to see you bullied because his basic nature is to protect, and he may become an ally against the macho man.

THERE'S A REASON THAT NICE GUYS FINISH LAST

I'd like to take a moment to thank the mothers of the men in the next category. They were brought up to open doors, watch a chick flick without complaining, and stop to change a damsel's flat tire in the rain. They're mama's good boy—they're nice guys and every woman should have one for a best friend (or a poker opponent). What he's looking for is a little appreciation. Boost his ego when he plays well against another opponent. Reward him with a smile if he checks to you with the best hand out of niceness. If he's to your right or left, gently make light (but brief) contact by touching his hand or shoulder. If he thinks you admire him, it's more likely you will be able to bluff him. If your bluff succeeds, don't ever show your hand; compliment him instead on how devilishly smart he was for folding. If your bluff doesn't succeed, also compliment him on his cleverness, because the right time will come to outwit him.

> "We haven't come a long way; we've come a short way. If we hadn't come a short way, no one would still be calling us 'baby.'"
>
> —Elizabeth Juneway

Another advantage to facing off Mr. Nice Guy is that you can always sweetly inquire, "Geesh, did you make a straight-draw on the **turn***?" The more your male opponent craves female attention, the more truthful he'll be. Manipulation via flirtation works best if you are perceived as being sweet or naive and not overly aggressive. Be aware that sometimes Mr. Nice Guy will check to you on the river with the best hand or call a bet instead of raising because he can't help being chivalrous. What a waste if you bet his hand for him when he was giving you a free ride. Mr. Nice Guys are all about saving bets that ordinarily you'd have to pay off, so don't forget to keep some nice-guy tender treats up your sleeve.

MEN WHO NEVER GET WRAPPED AROUND A PINKY

The most infuriating type of man is the one who doesn't suspect you're an inferior player because you're a woman and

***Turn—in hold 'em, the fourth community card dealt; in seven-card stud, the fourth card dealt to each player.**

treats you as an equal. He may or may not be misogynistic, but either way, he's too evolved and/or experienced to let ignorance affect his reasoning. Thank heavens there are not many men at the poker table who fall into this category. The reason we can outplay most men is that they fall prey to one or more of the following: they perceive us as vulnerable, underestimate our competitive strength, want to coddle and protect us, want to get in our pants, fear us, hate us, or are reminded by us of their mothers.

Don't get all bent out of shape if you're not respected as a female player. Chauvinism accounts for one of the reasons we have a financial advantage at the poker table. Playing poker is about making money and having financial independence, not about the passage of the Equal Rights Amendment.

TIP 32

Work on developing your intuitive skills.

Women are more accepting of drawing conclusions based solely on feelings than men are. This is why many men think women are illogical. But there are subliminal messages present at the poker table, and the quicker and more accurately you can pick up on them, the greater your advantage becomes. Sometimes when you feel something is going on but you don't know why, your

> It takes practice to know the difference between genuine insight and what is a projection of your own hopes or fears.

intuition could be in action. But you need to learn when that feeling is real and when it's just a hunch. It takes practice to know the difference between genuine insight and what is a projection of your own hopes or fears.

If you sit down at a roulette table and suddenly feel a strong urge to put money on No. 25 because you got married June 25, that's a hunch, not intuition. But if you go to lunch with your husband and he acts naturally, but nonetheless you feel something is wrong, that's intuition. You are intuiting that something is different because you know him so well. It's an air of change that no matter how hard he tries to conceal or suppress, you can detect. There is no concrete evidence; it is simply your intuition detecting a truth.

I don't think women are innately more intuitive than men, but I think they are more practiced at wanting to know what men are thinking. Traditionally in the male-female relationship, we have been relegated to a reactive position. Men for the most part are the initiators, and we are left analyzing with our girlfriends what they could be thinking. Men wonder, yes, but they aren't as determined as we are to solve the mystery of what goes on inside the brain of the opposite sex. They are more likely to throw up their hands, say, "Women are a mystery to me," roll over, and turn out the light.

A bud and I were walking through Caesar's poker room, and we stopped to watch a heads-up match between New York Marty and Connie Cupcake (two players who were frequently my opponents). After watching a few hands I said to my bud: "Connie looks unhinged. She's going to explode." My bud countered, "Nah—she looks like she always does." Two minutes later Connie picked up her drink and threw it in Marty's face.

Another time I was playing in a game with an old friend, Ira the Instigator, and he was provoking another player, Rudy, by making barbs after he won each hand. I whispered to Ira, "Rudy is right on the edge; be careful." Ira responded: "You don't understand. I know just how far to push my opponents." A few minutes later Rudy pulled Ira out of the chair by the nape of his neck and bit him violently on the back.

How was I able to sense these two conflagrations? I believe it comes from two things: caring what people are feeling and being practiced in observing human behavior. I am very sensitive to detecting anger in particular, because in many of my early relationships it was used as a means to control me.

I think most women consider themselves intuitive. It would be interesting to analyze why. Whatever the reason, intuition develops from being extremely sensitive to what a person is feeling. By simply paying close attention to how people behave, you can strengthen your intuitive powers. My suggestion for you at the poker table is to designate one player whom you encounter often and zero in on everything he says and does. Watch him the way a cat observes a bird—with intense concentration. See if you can predict any of his future movements. After a few days of watching, test your conclusions by trying to anticipate what he's going to do before he does it. When you've got him down

> "She had always been too wise to tell him all she thought and felt, knowing by some intuition of her own womanhood that no man wants to know everything of any woman."
>
> —Pearl S. Buck

> **Intuition and Poker**
>
> When we take our intuition to the poker table, we can see things about men that they can't detect in us. We can sense emotions that most men have been taught not to recognize, because it's unmanly and easier on the brain to leave unacknowledged. We can use this long-studied talent to read a player—and to beat him!

so well you even know when he's going to reach for his drink, do the same experiment with another regular player.

When you feel capable and comfortable with trusting your instincts, you'll also feel instilled with courage and confidence.

TIP 33

Give the impression that you are well-off (whether you are or not).

I stumbled on the knowledge that a man's confidence level is lowered if he thinks his female opponent owns an orchard of money trees. A player was chiding me about losing a big pot and, sick of it, I turned to him and said: "Big deal. My trust-fund check is due tomorrow." He was crestfallen that his barb didn't penetrate my nonchalant attitude.

He treated me more respectfully from that moment on, and I no longer experienced any annoying post-hand gloats.

Money—who has it and who doesn't—is the essence of poker power. You'll have a disadvantage if you play against someone who is mega-wealthy, because the only loss he ever suffers is pride. It's troubling to think that what to you is a big deal is peanuts to your opponent. So simply eliminate the disadvantage of financial inequality and make the world believe your maiden name was Rockefeller or anything you wish.

No one needs to know if you're an average Josephine who eats mac and cheese once a week to keep within her budget. You can still convey the image that you're four-star all the way and that you've never set foot inside a dollar store. My opponents have long believed that the limit I play is beneath me and that I spill more money in the streets each week than they make in a month. That's because of my knowledge of brands, style of dress, restaurant references, and general preferences for those things that are associated with the word "best."

> "Nothing is more intolerable than a wealthy woman."
>
> —Juvenal (A.D. 60)

How do you think your opponent feels if he needs to win the next pot to pay his rent, but to you winning or losing seems to make about as much difference as whether the sun sets at 5:45 P.M. or 5:47 P.M.? It lowers his confidence in his ability to outplay you, because the money is not as consequential to you as it is to him. I once won a pot from a nasty, financially strapped opponent and quipped, "Oh, goody, now I can send Sparky to doggie day care." He came up behind me later and whispered, "I'd like to kill you." I was a little unnerved but I retorted, "Stand in line."

How do you think your opponent feels if he needs to win the next pot to pay his rent, but to you winning or losing seems to make about as much difference as whether the sun sets at 5:45 P.M. or 5:47 P.M.?

If a woman obviously has money because she's playing high limit or has a diamond on her finger as big as a golf ball, a man's first—and usually only—thought is that she got the money from her husband. It stings him if she's being cared for by Daddy Warbucks, but if she's made her money on her own, it'll drive him *crazy.* Men evaluate a person's worth as a human being differently than women do; they feel inferior to anyone whose assets dwarf their own. I'm not suggesting out-and-out fabrication when you're creating your well-to-do image because that's creepy and, besides, the truly wealthy usually don't brag. Like putting on a dab of perfume, you want to just hint at being rich and use that image as a secret weapon against the phony chauvinistic opponent who needs to be shrunk down to size.

Don't Swallow Any Money Pits

While you're striving to create the impression of affluence, remember not to be intimidated by someone else's obvious wealth. If a player says he just made a killing in the stock market, don't plead for a stock tip. If he claims his horse just won the Kentucky Derby, make sure he can answer the question, "What state is the home of Churchill Downs?" I've had more men tell me they are producers than there are movie theatres. Such poppycock. Create an illusion, but don't fall for one.

But remember, there is a trade-off. If you are perceived as being dough-endowed, you must be extremely careful that you don't become a target for anyone following you home to rob you.

TIP 34

If a flirtatious woman sits down, take advantage of the changed dynamics.

Quoting a 32-year-old male World Poker Tour champion: "If I were a woman player, I'd dress like a slut and flirt my ass off. I'd be able to retire before I needed a breast lift."

Most men will vie for the attention of a flirtatious pretty woman in a poker game. If you are that woman, you can play one man against another by paying attention to only a favored few. The ignored guys will start seething and trying to outplay the favored guys. The favored guys will become distracted by the pretty girl's presence and will be enraptured by her attention versus the four queens in the deck. When I witness the tug-of-war among men for the attention of a pretty woman, I believe women don't control the world because we have chosen not to.

If you're outside of the center ring, don't let the prancing filly get under your skin. Her canyon cleavage is working for you by turning your male opponents into Silly Putty. Just focus on how her presence is changing the dynamics of the game and adjust your play to take into consideration show-offy maneuvers like an invalid reraise or a bluff on the river. Some men play better, becoming more aggressive, and some men play worse, wanting to win so badly to gain Flirty's favor that they can't fold. Old Gray George, who was put out to pasture 20 years ago, might suddenly start acting like a free-spirited stallion. The geek might strip off his pocket protector and glasses, regardless of whether he can still see the cards. But whatever happens, you should welcome the cute flirt to the game and get ready to stack chips, because some of the guys are going to lose their money faster trying to upstage one another. All you'll have to do is sit back with your purse open and enjoy the show.

TIP 35

Know how to take your opponents' temperatures.

Players' internal temperatures rise and fall depending upon a rise or fall of their chips, and it's your job to monitor everyone's health. Just as if you were a nurse on rounds, take each opponent's temperature regularly to assess who is feverishly hot, who is morgue chilly, who feels chip healthy, who looks ready to check out, or who has a tourniquet on too tightly. Bear in mind that a player's diagnosis can change abruptly, and you need to adapt your play accordingly. You can carve up a player ready for the morgue by check-raising and sucking out his remaining breaths, but you can't try to outplay the table surgeon when his ego has been recently promoted. The player with a fever who is on a suicide mission has to be called more liberally, and the player who has just dialed Dr. Kevorkian may throw off his chips with any hand to put himself out of misery. The player ready to check out by going home is playing tightly, so be certain your hand has quality value if you get involved. The only players who tend to stay consistent are the cuckoos on a day pass from the psychiatric wing.

Take each opponent's temperature regularly to assess who is feverishly hot, who is morgue chilly, who feels chip healthy, or who has a tourniquet on too tightly.

STAY ALERT

If you look up and there's a player sitting in seat No. 6 and you have no idea when he sat down, your own head needs examining. Always take note of who is making a **rebuy***, who is going postal, who is looking for revenge, and who is dreaming of happy hour. The table is in constant flux. The player who was hoping to play doctor with you one moment may be preparing you for a lethal injection the next. As long as you're at the table, you can't afford to go on a mental coffee break.

***Rebuy—purchasing more chips.**

TIP 36

Check-raise opponents who are complaining about their luck.

Whiners expect the worst of all possible results. If a fatalist player knows he's going to be **drawn out on***, he'll be anxiously waiting to muck his hand on each street. He wants to continue losing to prove to the table he's right, and for some bizarre reason he prefers the feelings associated with being unlucky. Check-raising the average player usually ensures a quick call, but check-raising the player who feels doomed to get unlucky can sometimes be a successful bluff because he's anxious to fold. Watch him carefully: Although he believes he's going to lose, he still may call. This technique should be used conservatively—if you get greedy, he will catch on. If you do get caught with your hand in the cookie jar, don't try bluffing him again because he'll call *every* time.

A player who feels like an unlucky loser is an ideal opponent, because both you and he want the same thing—for him to lose.

***Draw out on—the best hand gets beat by a secondary one.**

A player who feels like an unlucky loser is an ideal opponent, because both you and he want the same thing—for him to lose. Agree with the bellyacher and let him sink further into his pit of self-pity. Don't ever say anything encouraging like, "You're a good player; it'll turn itself around." Comfort him with country-and-western triteness, "Yup, Mr. Boo Hoo, if it weren't for bad luck, you'd have no luck at all."

7

Every Face Tells a Story (or How Botox Can Save You Money)

Tells— the Body Language of Poker

TIP 37

Strive to make all your motions the same so as not to reveal the strength of your hand through body language.

I recently watched a TV show called *Numbers* about a math professor who exposed the patterns of a serial killer using high-level mathematics. Although the killer carefully randomized his victims' locations, he still inadvertently left a pattern that the math wiz was able to detect. If a killer whose entire future depended upon deception failed at disguising his actions, what are your chances of fooling your opponents by firing chips into the pot fiercely one minute and placing them gently the next? A player who studies human behavior will discover your pattern, no matter how hard you try to act haphazardly. We are not Academy Award-winning actors who can transform ourselves into other characters; we are poker players, and our best bet is to act as much like a still-life bowl of fruit as possible.

Your goal should be to peek at your cards identically from one hand to the next, pause the same amount of time before executing a raise or calling a bet, keep your eyes focused on the ongoing action, protect the cards you're going to dump and the playable hands in the same fashion, slide your chips toward the pot at exactly the same speed and distance, breathe with ease, and all the while prevent any telling emotion from creeping onto your face. Once you perfect the Mona Lisa face, you'll be ready to pose for the next Leonardo or to get your Ph.D. in human behaviorism.

"The most common Tell is the pulse in a man's neck. . . . When you see a man's neck just throbbing away, you know he's excited, and usually he's excited because he is bluffing."

—Doyle Brunson
How I Made $1,000,000 Playing Poker

Also be aware of your posture and betting style. A relaxed player who is leaning back, chatting to a friend, is obviously less involved with his hand and more apt to fold. An attentive person sitting soldier straight with his eyes darting is more likely to stay in the action, if not to raise the pot himself.

If a player is gleefully chirping, he's less likely to be bluffing. It's difficult to bluff and chat simultaneously; it's like trying to fool a lie detector when you're guilty. On the other hand, if a person's face looks like he just viewed an open casket, he might be bluffing. If you have done some homework prior to the moment of trying to figure out whether a player is bluffing, you may have noticed a difference in his

Try to peek at your cards identically from one hand to the next, pause the same amount of time before executing a raise or calling a bet, and slide your chips toward the pot at exactly the same speed.

breathing pattern. Some people barely breathe when they bluff, and others can't help sucking in air. Phil Laak, who is nicknamed the "Unabomber," uses the funniest technique of all to disguise a bluff from a real bet. He takes the hood of his sweatshirt and pulls it tightly over his head so you can barely see any part of his face, except his sunglasses.

The crème de la crème of players can mix it up and manipulate an opponent into either calling or folding via a feigned expression or a leading comment, but they've had years of experience in testing what works and what doesn't. If you're a beginner, keep your mouth zipped when making a bet or you're likely to tip off your hand. But if your decision is whether to call or fold, do try to get your opponent to talk. Any question will do. His voice intonation often will be the additional help you need to make a correct call or fold. Conversely, remember that when your opponent tries to get you to talk, he has the same underlying motivation.

No matter whether you're a fresh face at the table or one with seasoned wrinkles, there is a player trying to get a tell on you. So never relax your defenses against successful players or even the ding-dong newcomers. The ability to read body language accurately doesn't belong just to the experts. One of my students, with only a few months of experience, pointed out that just before I made a bet, I always glanced at my chips. That was an ego bummer, but

Tells 101

Remember this: Often players will act the opposite of their intentions. A clashing splash of chips can actually mean I ain't got a damn thing, and a hesitant call accompanied by a sigh can indicate a monster hand. How to tell what's what? That takes years of playing and observing opponents. But one key thing to watch for is exaggeration–if the action seems melodramatic, it may be.

on reflection I realized she was right. Some smarty-pants players want to put you down by revealing a tell, but don't be miffed. Be pleased—the revelation will save you money.

TIP 38

Assess players by their actions, not their images.

The most deceptive and challenging player I know is Danny Robison. He looks like Krusty the Clown, is as good-natured as Santa Claus in January, is more probing than Ken Starr, and can simultaneously convert you to Christianity and bluff you. His nonstop nonsense can give you belly cramps from laughing, but all the while he is stacking your chips higher and higher. His style of play is so off-the-wall and his appearance so buffoonish that it's hard to think of him as a serious player, much less as a force to contend with. But he consistently outwits even those of us who are onto his act.

Don't be fooled by goofiness (or, for that matter, by milquetoast mild-manneredness or dumb-blonde ditziness or any other "acts" you encounter). Although Danny appears to be as intimidating as Elmer Fudd with a pop gun, he's as accurate as a calculator, reads tells better than The Amazing Kreskin, and is capable of creating interpersonal conflicts between lifelong friends. So judge your opponent not by his funny jokes, his silly outfit, or the Bible under his arm, but by how many hands he wins and how many players he sends home with empty pockets and bad-beat stories.

Judge your opponent not by his funny jokes, his silly outfit, or the Bible under his arm, but by how many hands he wins and how many players he sends home with empty pockets and bad-beat stories.

Another lovable character who has managed to fool many in the poker world is Artie Cobb. He's known for entering tournaments wearing fake buck teeth, chicken-head hats, and other ridiculous paraphernalia that sends the message, "I'm just silly—don't give me a second thought." But as Artie started winning tournament after tournament, we had to look past the nutty props and realize that he's an expert player who's been deceiving us to his advantage.

What you see is often not what you get. A guy who looks like Vin Diesel may actually be afraid of his own mother's shadow, and the bloke whose appearance suggests he resides in a subway tunnel may in fact own 100,000 shares of Microsoft stock. Make your judgments about an opponent from the way he plays his hands, not from the image he's hoping will dupe you. But try to turn the tables and use the mistakes men make so often regarding women to your advantage. Just because you appear to be a gentle blonde joshing with a sexy Southern accent or a sweet, girl-next-door novice playing for fun doesn't mean that inside your brain you can't be as calculating as a shark at dinnertime.

TIP 39

Watch your opponents' hands and eyes.

We've all seen the World Poker Tour players on television wearing their dark mirrored or googly-eyed glasses* to conceal their eyes. It's not because they all have extremely sensitive eyes (or wish their brown eyes were blue), but rather because they're trying to hide either their tells or the fact that they're staring at their opponents. Did your mama ever tell you, "It's impolite to stare"? Well, forget that advice. In poker, it's part of the game and you must get over any qualms about etiquette. There's valuable information in a poker player's eyes and hands, and it's your job to get it.

***There is currently a controversy about whether a player should be allowed to wear sunglasses, because concealing expressions is part of the art of the game.**

For example, if a player stares at the flop waiting for it to turn into a frog prince, it usually means nothing good has happened. When a player rechecks his hole cards, he either has forgotten the suits or is trying to make you think he has.

> "Almost all gamesters learn to control their faces. . . . The hand blabs secrets shamelessly."
>
> —Stephan Zweig
> *Four-and-Twenty Hours in a Woman's Life*

An old geezer I played stud with at the Mirage enacted this same tell for 10 years. Each time his flush was already completed, he made an obvious point of looking back at his cards to make you believe he wasn't there yet. Fool me once . . .

Another reliable tell is when a player acts as if something behind the table is of great interest, such as the cocktail waitress's behind or an amazing putt being replayed on the TV, and then—boing—it's his turn and he quickly raises or reraises with newfound interest. If you've **limped*** into this hand with marginal hopes, giddyup out. If you were the initial raiser, proceed with caution and be prepared to pull the plug on the next card.

Always keep your hands off of your face and out of your mouth. First, the guy whose chips you're stacking may not have washed his hands after his last restroom stop. Second, a savvy player will detect that you're bluffing if you suddenly cover your mouth when usually you don't. Also, a hand fussing with a face often indicates anxiety. Try to be consistent with your hand movements, whether you're going to fold, call, raise, or just keep showing off your new 2-carat engagement ring.

Don't jump to conclusions. Once when I was playing seven-card stud eight-or-better, a pal commented: "Did you notice

*Limped—**simply called the opening bet.**

how Ernie's hands shake when he makes a bet? He's scared and doesn't have a thing." The truth was, Ernie may have been scared, but that's not why his hands were trembling. I happened to know he had a neurological disorder. Unless you've accumulated notes on a particular player, don't assume shaky hands are an obvious tell of weakness. In some cases, yes, he's a scaredy-cat wimp, but at other times that tremble might indicate that his card-hand is gargantuan. Or, sadly, he may just have palsy.

There's valuable information in a poker player's eyes and hands, and it's your job to get it.

Note that inexperienced players keep their hole cards guarded with their hands when they intend to play, but when they hold trashy cards, they overanxiously zip them into the muck. I've even seen someone be so overt as to put her good-luck charm on top of her cards when she intended to play, but left them unprotected when she didn't.

Sometimes I find that staring at a man who is upset from losing may provoke him to act more aggressively. It could be cultural defiance or a reflex action at being scrutinized at an unflattering moment. If you have the type of hand you'd like to tiptoe to the river with, don't be overt in your eye contact. But if your hand is a big favorite, bet, stare into your opponent's face, and never cry uncle. Your heart might

Get Real

In your eagerness to discover an advantage through a tell, don't make up one that doesn't exist. Sometimes an itchy ear is only an itchy ear. Don't rationalize and waste bets. Be patient.

be doing the Charleston in double time from the intense stare-down but you've got to have guts, girlfriend, to get the cash flowing from his stack to yours.

TIP 40

Reaction time can reveal the nature and strength of your hand.

How long it takes someone to react to a certain event is telling. Think about this example from life: Marsha asks John to marry her. John covers her with kisses and murmurs passionately over and over, "Yes, yes. I thought you'd never ask." Marsha obviously can construe that John is happy, and with no lapse in response time, "yes" rings as true as their future wedding bells.

The same couple two years earlier: Just after John asks Marsha to marry him, her cell phone rings. She answers it and begins chatting about the police officer who asked her sister out for a date. Only after her five-minute cell conversation concludes does she turn back to John and ask, "Now what was it you were saying?" It is logical for John to infer that Marsha's delayed reaction time signifies that she is not anxious to marry. This is all obvious, yes? Well, similar conclusions can be drawn from a person's reaction time in poker, especially if you factor in expressions and body language.

In Mike Caro's *Book of Tells* he offers two valuable laws. The first is: *If a player looks and then checks instantly, it's unlikely he has improved his hand.* To understand this better, imagine you are drawing to an ace-high diamond flush. You know that your opponent knows you're drawing, and he knows that you know he knows. You don't mull over the possibilities when you miss; you immediately check because you know he will call if you bet. On the other hand, if you catch the ace of spades, giving you a pair of aces, you will pause to consider whether one pair of aces is the best hand. Your pause sends the message that you have something to think over.

The second law is: *If a player looks and then bets instantly, it's unlikely he's bluffing.* Using the same example, you peek at your river card and discover you've made the flush. If you're like most players, you bet automatically. Notice how your body suddenly relaxes, which can be visibly detected by an astute player.

One aspect of Mike's discussion on reaction time is that bluffing usually requires a hesitation to evaluate whether it will be successful. I do not wholly agree. If your opponent is on tilt, he could fire those chips in automatically when you check. Or if a man has been passively calling a woman player on the previous streets, he may instantaneously feel a surge of testosterone and come out betting without mulling over the consequences. If you have been following the ups and downs of your opponents' moods, your own course of action becomes easier.

PATIENCE IS A VIRTUE

One generalization Mike makes is: "You can figure that players who won't look until they *must* are likely to need improvement." Would you think just the opposite? Mike is a genius, but he's not totally mad*, because his powers of observation on human behavior are often right on. For example, in seven-card stud Joan raises with a queen showing, and Raquel reraises with buried aces. Joan hesitates but then calls. (Joan knows she may be playing catch-up, because Raquel is a solid player). On fifth street Joan pairs her fourth street card and now has two sixes, as well as two queens. She bets her two pair, and Raquel calls (correctly). On sixth street Joan bets; Raquel still has not made two pair and (correctly) calls again. The dealer pitches the river cards. Raquel holds her breath, watching as Joan peeks at her last card. Only when Joan checks will Raquel look at her card, praying for a second pair or a third ace.

Mike's conclusion is: "Players who must improve to win are in more suspenseful situations than those who feel they might already have a winning hand. That's important, because players in suspenseful situations are likely to wait before looking; players in low-pressure situations are apt to look right away." This may sound counterintuitive, but it makes perfect sense to a card player who wants to watch his opponent's reaction first before getting the good or bad news about his own hand.

You may have wondered when you watch the pros on television why they take so long to fold when they hold absolute bupkus. It's just part of disguising their hands to

***Mike Caro's nickname is the "Mad Genius."**

withhold information. Suppose you made a miscalculated bluff and get raised. If you fold immediately, it's obvious your bet was a bluff. No one wants his opponent to know he was just successfully picked off. The same is true if you have a powerhouse and get raised. If you react immediately and reraise, you're revealing that your hand is so big it doesn't even require thought. That makes it much easier for your opponent to fold. The issue of reaction time is simple in one way and complicated in another, but following the basic rule of slowing down to avoid giving your opponent information is overall good advice.

Suppose you made a miscalculated bluff and get raised. If you fold immediately, it's obvious your bet was a bluff. No one wants his opponent to know he was just successfully picked off.

8

If All Is Not Lost, Where Is It?

A Closer Look at Why Your Win Rate May Be Below Par

TIP 41

The only person who can effectively beat you is you.

If you take two equally skilled players, the player who can let go of a mistake quicker will outearn the player who beats herself up for making an error. What happens when you abuse yourself for being stupid? You get stuck in the past.

Poker is a game that moves forward rapidly, and sometimes your emotional stability can't keep pace. If you're wallowing in a hand played 10 minutes ago, it is difficult to make clear decisions about the hands you're playing now. Sometimes you'll be given a reprieve by fate, and a good hand won't arrive until you've finished self-flagellating. But other times your next playable hand will turn up as you're watching your chips being stacked up by the giggling tourist.

OK, it's true you tried to bluff the buffoon who never folds any hand on the river. Yes, that was bad judgment, especially since you'd even told yourself when you sat down, *don't bluff* the rich guy whose curiosity always gets the best of him. So what was wrong with you? How could you be so stupid? You *idiot.* Dope. Moron. Are you feeling bad enough yet? No? You cretin! Dunderhead! Nitwit! I hope your ego is deflated by now, because I'm running out of synonyms for dumbhead. If you're the type who lambastes herself for a mistake, ask yourself, what does it accomplish? Aside from making me happy, because you're just the type of player I want to size up against—someone who feels she doesn't deserve to win.

Everything you did to mentally prepare yourself for today's poker session—the exercise, the meditation, screening your calls, driving at the speed limit—has been erased. And who pushed the button that set off the explosion of self-loathing? No, not your mother. You did.

> "Always remember, the first thing a gambler has to do is make friends with himself."
>
> —Pug Pearson

You might have temporarily forgotten that every poker player goofs up at one time or another: outthinks herself, misreads a tell, becomes too aggressive for the situation, neglects to bluff, or even thinks she has a diamond when it's a heart. It's highly unlikely that even a professional could finish any session without acknowledging at least one error in judgment.

Your objective is to put as much distance between your mistakes as possible. If you made the goof-up of becoming overly tired but continued to play on January 15th, you will make the same error again, but let's hope it's not on January 16th. Every mistake at poker provides a valuable lesson that can improve your game. But the time to review that lesson is not while you're still at the table trying to concentrate; it's after you've left the cashier's cage.

If you didn't learn to "let go" easily as a child, it's time to learn it as an adult. It's a tall order, but any character flaw can be either eliminated or greatly reduced. The key is to identify your weaknesses and actively work on trying to eradicate the negative aspects of your personality that affect your game.

Have you got that through your noggin, or do you need to hear it again? *The only person who can effectively beat you is you!*

TIP 42

If you start feeling gun-shy from a series of bad beats, go home (or to the bar).

Any player can recover from one bad beat. But successfully recovering from a series of rotten breaks is what separates the girls from the women. After you aggressively (and correctly) bet your high two pair three times and got raised by players who made, respectively, an inside-straight, three **ducks***, and a **backdoor flush****, it

***Duck—nickname for a deuce.**
****Backdoor flush—a hold 'em example: Your two starting cards are K-Q of hearts, the flop is K(♦), 3(♠), 2(♥), the turn and river are both hearts. You inadvertently made a flush by catching perfectly on the remaining two betting rounds. This is also known as coming through the backdoor.**

would be unusual for your confidence not to feel frayed. Your stack has suddenly shrunk from small winner to big loser faster than your hair frizzes in humidity. I feel your pain, sister. Gosh, you don't even want to be dealt a playable hand until you catch your breath, but you look down and, good grief, there's another pair of cocky kings. Marvin the Maniac, who raises nine out of 10 pots, raises again with an ace showing. Normally you'd reraise to isolate the play between just you and him, but you're feeling a little unnerved and decide to call. A player to your left who wouldn't have called two bets with a three-flush calls the single raise and, criminy, seat Nos. 5, 6, and 7 also call with God knows what. What a barrel of pickles this hand has turned into.

Mistakes will compound themselves, and just like animals, poker players can smell fear and will pounce on the player acting weak and injured with the same ferocity as a hungry lion leaping onto a limping gazelle.

What could have been a highly advantageous situation, your kings versus the maniac's ace-high, has turned into a six-handed free-for-all. This is the last thing you wanted to happen with a big pair. On fourth street Chip-Burner Charlie pairs his door-card four and bets the maximum. Marvin the Maniac raises, and you have no idea where you're at. How did this happen?

Here's how: You became gun-shy on third street and failed to make the proper reraise, because you feared you'd lose another hand. You are now playing a losing game. Unless you can pull yourself together and stop being a wimp, it's best to pack it in for the day. Mistakes will compound themselves, and just like animals, poker players can smell fear and will pounce on the player acting weak and injured with the same ferocity as a hungry lion leaping onto a limping gazelle.

Doesn't a martini sound good about now, especially when the alternative is a pack of sharp-toothed players fighting over who's going to take your money next? Get up, wounded gazelle. I'm buying.

TIP 43

Do not develop a personal vendetta against a particular player.

The first thing a beginner must do is concentrate on her own hand. The next thing she needs to consider is what her opponent may hold. When she's got these down, she should take into account what he thinks she has. Once she's got all this figured out, she must evaluate what her opponent thinks she thinks he has. This is an endless cycle, but it doesn't matter what he thinks she thinks he thinks she thinks if he's not actually thinking at all, but instead is raising simply because he specifically wants to beat her. Maybe it's because she has purple hair or a nose ring, or she beat him the last five hands and it's intolerable

Your Fight, Their Gain

Don't expect other players to act as referees to help cool down a rivalry. Pros feed off ongoing feuds between players. It works to their advantage when two people act overly aggressive with each other for the sake of one-upmanship. The pros simply can join the fray with the best hand and let the feuding players build big pots. And it's the nature of man (especially of men) to enjoy watching people beat on each other. But you aren't at the table to bring enjoyment to your opponents waiting eagerly for a TKO, so stay relaxed and don't get involved in a table rivalry.

to lose to a woman. Poker is complicated psychology, even without adding a personal conflict into the mix.

There will be players whom you don't like, and there will be players who don't like you, even if you sit there as innocent as Sleeping Beauty. Sometimes you have no control over how a player feels about you (especially if you actually were born with purple hair). But you can somewhat control how you feel about another player. If he's a swaggering bully who spews vitriol and brags he just got out of jail for wife abuse, you may not be able to prevent an adverse reaction. But if his only offense is that he just beat you with an inferior hand in the last five pots you played together, fuhgettaboutit—you outplayed him and there's a good chance he'll lose those chips back (ideally to you).

DON'T RISE TO THE BAIT

I played against someone who thought he was so superior to me that he challenged me to an IQ test. At first I took the bait and said, "You betcha—where's the closest Mensa office?"

But then I realized that engaging in this challenge—no matter what the outcome—would further complicate our table relationship, and it was already difficult enough. Whether I won or lost the bet, the emotional conflict between us would escalate to a level at which I no longer would be able to deduce the true meaning of a raise. Is he raising because his hand is superior, or because my IQ is higher? Or is he raising because his IQ is higher, and he believes that is enough to beat me? Whenever you can avoid it, don't add interpersonal issues to an already complicated formula.

It's hard enough to control the sting of losing a hand to a neutral opponent, but if you've lost to Public Enemy No. 1, your disappointment will spill over into other hands with other opponents.

A personal vendetta will affect not only the way you play against your foe, but also how you play against the other players. It's hard enough to control the sting of losing a hand to a neutral opponent, but if you've lost to Public Enemy No. 1, your disappointment will spill over into other hands with other opponents. You'll be more likely to go on tilt or to get distracted by rooting so hard against your foe when you're not even in the hand. Rooting against a particular player saps energy, and if you're actually a nice person, it doesn't make you feel too great about yourself.

I believe that women are more vulnerable to being affected by a feud than men are because most of us care deeply about how a person feels about us, even if we don't like him. Stay on the sunny side of the street and outside of the boxing ring, where you might end up on the ropes.

TIP 44

Don't telegraph when you are giving up on a hand.

There are a variety of ways people telegraph their intentions to fold: by picking up their cards and getting poised to muck, by turning away from their hands, or by showing obvious disinterest, to name just a few. You may already know why doing so is unfair to the players to your left—knowing you are about to fold makes it easier for the players on your right to raise. But have you ever thought of the other reason to conceal your intention to discard? If you consistently indicate when you're going to fold, it then becomes obvious when you're going to call or raise. If your opponents have that information, they will be less likely to attempt a **steal*** or to play a marginal hand. This is Basic Poker 101.

If you consistently indicate when you're going to fold, it then becomes obvious when you're going to call or raise.

Some players lack the patience to wait their turns, so stay tuned to the body language of your opponents on the left. It's not necessary to chastise them for playing out of turn, because you are gaining the opportunity to steal right through them. During each hand, practice trying to detect whether your opponents intend to

***Steal—to win the antes or the blinds by bluffing.**

fold or play before it's their turn to act. Being ultra-aware can save bets and earn extra money. We're supposed to be the intuitive sex—let's hone this skill and our male opponents will start believing we're psychic!

TIP 45

When you're losing, do not jump into a higher game to get even.

Every casino should have a cliff outside the entrance, so a person who has been losing would have at least four options: 1) to get even in the game she originally played and lost, 2) to go home, 3) to jump up to a higher level, or 4) to jump off the cliff. There's only a modicum of difference between options No. 3 and No. 4, as far as your emotional stability at the time of the decision.

> "Don't swim beyond your depth, though."
>
> —Leo Tolstoy
> *War and Peace*

When you are so battered that the only way you can relieve the pain is to take the jump upward, stop and consider the possible outcomes. You might think there's a 50-percent chance you'll pull out even. Alas, you're way off. If you sit down at a higher-stakes table and act wild, the upper-limit players are just going to swallow you whole and burp you into the parking lot. If you sit down and wait for a big hand, you've got a plan at least, but it's a transparent one. Good players will still be able to outplay you, because when you have nothing and they have nothing, they will take the pots, and when you have something, they'll know it and get out of the way.

It is true that sometimes the higher-limit games are juicier than the game in which you dug your hole. Say you do get even this time and refill your grave. What are you going to do the next time your backhoe starts chomping the earth beneath you? Of course, the same thing—you've tricked yourself into believing there's always a way out before the coffin lid closes. It might just work a couple of times, but eventually that grave digger is going to cover you with earth and worms. What happens when the higher limit isn't one rung above, but two or three? So instead of playing $20/$40, your way out is at $80/$160. Your comfort level is going to be strung so tightly that your opponents will hear you ping.

The next time you play, you buy in to your normal game with relief. But, oh no, it seems a bit boring, doesn't it? You

Russian Roulette at the Poker Table

Players who up their stakes when they are losing to get even may as well pick up a gun, put one bullet in the chamber, and start clicking. It's insanity to step up your game when your head is emotionally whacked from suffering a big loss. You're on tilt before you even play your first hand.

don't want to play at the minion table. You're a big girl now. The craving for a bigger adrenaline rush will manipulate your logic until you're buying in again at a limit that will make your bankroll nauseated. At some point the card goddess is going to say, "Patooie. If this chick wants action, fasten your seatbelt, honey." And that's when you'll go broke in one session and feel a world of pain.

Once more, because this point deserves repeating, if your game plan is in place before you enter the casino and you are a smart girl, you won't make irrational spontaneous decisions, such as going past your stop-loss limit, playing all night, or stepping up to a bigger game when you're emotionally ill-prepared.

TIP 46

As a beginner, never show your hand, especially not after a bluff or to gain sympathy for a bad beat.

This will happen to you over and over again, even after you've been playing for 20 years: First, you lose trip aces to the guy on your right; 10 minutes later you fail to make a flush and he wins with one pair. The third hand he's involved in (when you're an onlooker), he takes a beat, turns to you upset, shows you his kings, laments his bad luck, and waits for you to say, "There, there, little man, Mama has a Band-Aid." He will have no recollection that he's asking for sympathy from the same person he triumphantly beat twice in the last half hour.

Players are silly that way. And you'll be silly, too, if you do the same thing. Opponents are not going to simultaneously try to get your money and extend sympathy when you lose. That's not part of their job description. Therefore, restrain yourself from giving away free information about your hand because you crave sympathy.

Opponents are not going to simultaneously try to get your money and extend sympathy when you lose.

Another time you'll likely be eager to reveal your hand is when you successfully bluff a big-ego opponent and want to show off that you're a smarty-pants. Don't do it. No one is going to break out in applause; what all of the observant players are going to think is, ah, when that hand comes up again, she is capable of bluffing. We don't want our opponents to realize what our bluffing capabilities are, because if they do, it's less likely those bluffs will work in the future.

You might see an experienced player show off a bluff, but usually it means that she has a plan for how that tip-off may trick an opponent in the future or put him on immediate tilt. As a beginner, you are probably not savvy enough yet to accurately calculate a future reaction when you tangle with this same player. Believe me, if you show a bluff, your chances of bluffing him again are close to zero, and he's going to be so anxious for revenge that you'll be forced to call him with all types of marginal hands. Yikes! You're going to regret changing the dynamics of the game, because you've turned a semi-predictable equation into one where you have less power to solve it.

TIP 47

Going on tilt can annihilate your win rate.

Tilting in a poker game means having a heated, illogical quarrel with yourself. You're completely off center, and whether you raise or call has no relation to what your chances of winning might be. In short, you're nutso—the hand that's throwing in the chips isn't connecting to the brain. Sometimes you can identify your irrational state, and sometimes you don't even bother to analyze why your chips are bouncing off the table. A tilt may last for one hand, or until you don't have any chips left and are digging into your pockets. You may even win a hand and still be on tilt.

A tilt may last for one hand, or until you don't have any chips left and are digging into your pockets. You may even win a hand and still be on tilt.

How does it happen? There are many causes. Some are related to a series of bad beats, or perhaps someone

The Lure of Gambling from Behind

A friend once heard a player say, "I'm going to treat myself to a tilt." What he meant was "I'm going to play a hand I shouldn't, but I might get lucky." It's similar to when you've been on a diet for a long time and then indulge in a hot fudge sundae. But while occasionally straying from your diet is no big deal, in poker it's necessary to play every hand to the best of your ability. Trying to beat the odds can be tempting, but remember, if you knowingly play a hand with negative **expectation*** it cuts into your earnings.

***Expectation—in the long run, the average profit or loss of a particular bet.**

made you angry and you lost control, or it may even be for reasons outside of poker. Being on tilt feels like being suspended in time between falling off a 500-foot ledge and going splat on the cement.

You might get away with chasing kings with a pair of sevens and make two pair by passively calling each street. But what if you don't just call? Suppose you attempt to outplay your opponent by raising on fifth street because he called you "clueless." Gosh darn it. He didn't fall for it; he raised you again. Doesn't he know who you are? Raise him back to teach him some respect! The end of this story isn't pretty, and by the way, you truly might be clueless. That hand will cost you more in expectation, because the reraise isn't going to cause him to lay down his hand, and he'll bet right back into you if he makes an open pair.

How badly you tilt and how often you tilt will determine the extent of disastrous effects on your win rate. If you have concluded that you earn one big bet an hour, two losing tilts in a session could cost you a huge amount of **equity***, possibly your entire earn for the day. If you're cognizant enough to realize you're on tilt, get your butt out of the chair until you're vertical again.

TIP 48

If you're losing after eight hours of play, quit.

Your back hurts after eight hours of being in the chair. Your eyes are strained. You've been mucking so many hands that you're developing carpal tunnel syndrome. Feeling a little frustrated? I'll bet you are. Uh, oh, a neighbor just made a snide remark that someone should check and see if you still have a pulse. Now you play a bad hand. And another. It's the snowball effect. When you are losing over a long period of time, your judgment becomes impaired, your image of strength goes all to hell, and strong and weak players alike will attempt to outplay you, because they think you couldn't win a hand if you picked your cards out of the deck. Now is the time to heed the words of Scarlett O'Hara: "Tomorrow is another day."

I always want my opponents to perceive me as a winner; as someone who never loses. The longer I stay at the table

***Equity—your expected value in a pot.**

bleeding or as dead weight, the easier it is for my opponents to reconsider that impression. But if I retreat when my eyes are glassing over, when I return the next day, my opponents are more likely to recall their first impression: "Oh, no. It's that darn Cat again, prancing in with her tail in the air."

Long ago I decided to quit after eight hours of play when things aren't going my way. I know my limits of concentration, and yours might be more or less. But eight hours is a long time to concentrate when you're stuck because of the additional stress you experience. So think carefully before you play longer than that. I don't care if the king of Sheba just sat down with a suitcase full of cash. There was a reason your mother told you to get out of the swimming pool when your lips had turned blue and your skin was all goose-bumpy. But you don't have mama to watch over you at the table and advise when enough is enough. You have only yourself. Instead of trying to decide whether to go or stay when you're losing, a preset maximum-hour rule can save money and your winning image.

> "This is where I should have quit, but some kind of strange sensation built up in me, a kind of challenge to fate, a kind of desire to give it a flick on the nose, or stick my tongue at it."
>
> —Fyodor Dostoevsky
> *The Gambler*

9

Do Not Mix Stripes and Plaids on a Blind Date (Not Even with Stevie Wonder)

How to Avoid Thinking or Acting Like an Amateur

TIP 49

Don't ever tell an opponent (even a friendly one) why you played a particular hand as you did.

- Would a policeman share his bullets with a robber who inadvertently left his at home?
- Would the Pillsbury Doughboy give away his secret for flaky rolls?
- Would you give diet tips to the gal who's determined to seduce your boyfriend?

Get the idea? All information on your playing strategies that you share willingly with an opponent provides insight on how to beat you in future hands. I don't care whether he's your boyfriend and he just gave you a puppy with a ruby collar for a birthday present. Next week you may find out he was doing more than smooching with the stripper at his best friend's bachelor party. And even if he's a true prince, why teach him how to beat you at your favorite game?

Be the player who gives up the least to learn the most.

Winning streaks and relationships don't necessarily last. If you always slow-play buried aces when a king raises, or if you always raise a four-flush on fourth street in last position, don't give away those secrets for free. (And by the way, you shouldn't always be playing any hand in the same way; "always" is not part of a poker player's vocabulary.) But whatever your strategies are, that's for you to know and me to find out.

DON'T BE GOADED

You will be most tempted to reveal your playing motivation when your opponent makes a sarcastic remark, such as, "What do you expect from a girl!" Defending yourself is wrong, because it makes you look unsure of yourself and may relay something valuable about the way you think. Armor yourself against the opinions of others. The critical loudmouth is a fool and obviously has a hard time controlling his emotions. The best way to pull his strings is to laugh at him. Men loathe being laughed at by a woman. Or if that's not your style, ignore him.

Sometimes it's just interesting to analyze the dynamics of a particular hand with the other players at the table. If you talk in the abstract, I don't see any harm, because sometimes to learn something you have to give up something. Just be the player who gives up the least to learn the most.

TIP 50

Do not become obsessed with getting even.

Have you ever taken a flight in coach from Los Angeles to New Zealand? It's a 22-hour flight. If you get on the plane already wishing you were landing in Auckland, you're going to have a grueling time. That's the same miserable feeling you'll have if the only thought that goes through your mind when you're losing is: *must* get even, *must* get even. It makes more sense to enjoy the journey.

> "I have seen a pregnant woman stand at a 21 game, oblivious to labor pains, until we thought we were going to become midwives, and leave only when we summoned an ambulance."
>
> —Harold S. Smith Sr.
> *I Want to Quit Winners*

People who get hung up on having to get even before they quit can find themselves playing all night, or even for days. At the end of the day, they could have taken a $40 loss, but instead they have to suck it up and write minus $1,500 in their record books.

It's just as important to minimize your losses as it is to maximize your wins. If you played well but couldn't pair up those aces in a crucial spot or failed to make that flush in a $2,000 pot, oh well, you did the best you could. Whether you win or lose, as long as you can say at the day's end, "I played every hand as well as I knew how," you had a productive day.

The mistake committed most often by really good pros is overestimating their ability to play when they're tired. Many a big-name player has crashed and burned her entire bankroll in one session because of the obsession to get even. If you can master this one small improvement in your attitude, you will suddenly make leaps in your game and gain the respect, and perhaps the envy, of the other players.

It's just as important to minimize your losses as it is to maximize your wins.

TIP 51

Don't set unrealistic expectations in relation to winning.

Much as you wish it were so, Johnny Depp isn't going to swish through your front door in a pirate costume anytime soon, and you're not going to win every session you play. Be psychologically prepared to lose without having to call the suicide hotline when you get home. There isn't a professional player, a poker author, or even a low-down **shot-taker*** who wins every time she plays.

***Shot-taker—one who cheats in order to win.**

Another error an amateur makes is to play poker to earn a certain amount of money that day. Maybe she wants to buy a new stereo or to take her honey out to a nice dinner, and she needs to win a specific amount of money to feel psychologically entitled to do so. But earning money at poker is a long-run venture. You aren't going to earn your calculated hourly win rate in a seven-hour session. You may win twenty times that amount, or you might lose five stereos and seven candlelit dinners in any one session. All you can do is arrive at the table mentally prepared for anything. You may find yourself stacking chips to the ceiling or reaching into your purse for a third buy-in.

TIP 52

Do not play with a short stack in a limit game.

Playing with a two-inch short stack of chips is as pathetic as wearing orthopedic shoes to a salsa club. Image, darling, image! Don't buy in for the table minimum and don't play with a dwindling stack that makes it obvious to everyone, including the **eye-in-the-sky***, that you are a loser. Of course, the amount of chips is a mere illusion. A player who is winning big may have converted some of his

***Eye-in-the-sky—the ceiling security camera.**

chips into cash and committed a no-no by pocketing the loot. (All winnings should remain on the table in clear view.) In contrast, a player who is surrounded by skyscraper stacks may appear to be the big table winner, but in fact he's made several buy-ins and he's big-time stuck. The truth is, opponents make more mistakes against players with big stacks and fewer mistakes against players with short stacks.

No matter what the situation, you want to keep the perception of your confidence intact—even to the garrulous passerby who readily provides unsolicited positive or negative press. We want a friend who comes up to the table to enviously remark, "Hey, Angie, do you *ever* lose?" We don't want her to announce, "Wow, Angie, did you drive here in a dump truck?" Your opponents will be as happy to learn you're on a losing streak as you'd be to find out your ex-husband's bride has a chronic case of plantar warts. We don't want happy opponents; we want opponents envious or on edge.

Your opponents will be as happy to learn you're on a losing streak as you'd be to find out your ex-husband's bride has a chronic case of plantar warts.

When you are perceived as a winner, you'll feel confident, other players will respect your authority at the table, and you'll play better regardless of your buy-in position. Some players will remember that you've double dipped into your wallet, but others won't, and the new players who arrive after you've refueled will sigh and be resigned to the fact that you are winning again.

When I am short-stacked and go all in (bet the remainder of my chips) on an early street, there are fewer opportunities for errors. That gives both me and my opponent an advantage. But I don't believe what I gain in dollars as the short stack is worth the hit to long-range images. If I am theoretically the superior player, I need to provide as many opportunities for opponent error as possible by having enough chips to bet every street. The stack-size issue is debatable among experts, but the majority lean in my direction: big stack good—small stack very bad. I know I don't want to look as if I'll be foraging in a dumpster by flashlight for dinner because I never made two pair all day.

Nevertheless, the upside of being all in is that you have no fear of being bluffed, because all of your investment is already in the pot. Plus you get extra value in the blinds when you don't have to call additional bets to play out the hand. But with very few chips, your bluffing potential is minimized. A hand you could have won outright by the fear of future bets is lost, because your opponent understands the advantage of calling an all-in player owing to pot odds.

The one undeniable joy of being short-stacked is that the railbirds are less likely to ask to borrow money.

The one undeniable joy of being short-stacked is that the **railbirds*** are less likely to ask to borrow money, which leads us to my next tip.

***Railbirds—often broke players or players who have busted out of the game. They literally hang on the rail separating the high-limit games from the low-limit ones like birdies on a high wire.**

TIP 53

Do not loan money to anyone whose name you just learned last week.

True story: A bum rat to whom I had never spoken approached me in the casino and said, "Jesus, your hair looks bad today." Without a pause, he then asked if I would loan him $200 so we could go halfsies in a tournament. It was one of the easiest propositions to turn down I've ever encountered. I replied, "When my hair looks good again, don't ask me then either."

It's not always easy to say no. I admit sheepishly that I was once successfully hit up for a loan by a player whose name I didn't know. I did know that he played the big game daily and owned a Jaguar dealership. Did I mention that he looked as if he worked out and was cute enough to be married to a movie star? What could a measly $400 mean to this stud? Of course he was going to pay me back. Well, the money must have meant more to him than I thought, because the next day he was still playing the big game but had no recollection of the loan, and said he'd call security if I ever asked again. From then on, each time I saw him playing a limit I couldn't afford, while I sat grinding out $50 an hour in a smaller game, it miffed me so much that my glasses would steam up.

There are professional con men out there who look at women as easy marks. And sometimes they're right. My girlfriend Sharon, who plays in $100/$200 games, ran out of money one day and was leaving the table to go to the bank when another player said: "Sweetie, here's twenty K; the game is too good to leave. I know you're good for it. You can pay me back tomorrow." Very appreciative of his trust and generosity, Sharon paid him back promptly the next day.

A few days later he came over to her and asked, "Honey, I'm running a little unlucky. Can you float me a twenty-four-hour loan?" He had been so kind to her, how could she say no under the circumstance? When he refused to pay her back, Sharon had no recourse. She couldn't beat him up, and she's not the type to hire someone who would; the con-man creep had counted on that. She did get loads of sympathy, but most of it went something like this: "How could you loan that scumbag money? Everyone knows he's a thief!"

You actually can feel the air change when somebody who is going to ask for a loan approaches, in the same way you can hear a snake part the grass.

SISTER, CAN YOU SPARE A DIME?

You actually can feel the air change when somebody who is going to ask for a loan approaches, in the same way you can hear a snake part the grass. By and large, as women we are easier targets, because generally it's harder for us to say no and we're the more compassionate gender. Some sad stories are hard to resist, such as, "I just want to buy a Christmas gift for my kid." And if the amount requested is small compared to the limit you're playing, you feel like Ebenezer Scrooge saying, "Tough luck."

My funniest story about being asked for money features a woman who thinks I'm someone else. I saw her coming, sensed the doom, and scurried out the back exit of the casino to avoid hearing the inevitable bad-beat stories. When I was in the parking lot, a car pulled out and bumped me in the leg. I yelled, "Hey, watch out! You just hit me!" The car stopped, the same woman I was avoiding opened the door, and while I was still rubbing my leg, she asked, "Janice, can you loan me two thousand until tomorrow?" I said: "Wait here. The money is in my car. I'll be right back with it." Zoom, zoom, zoom, zoom.

> "Losing as much money as I can get hold of is an instant solution to my economic problems."
>
> —Lucien Freud

There will be times when you are more vulnerable to the pleas—it's your birthday, you just took a big win, or you genuinely feel sorry for the guy because he's got a good heart. My advice is to treat all loans as gifts. If you're feeling generous and you don't know someone else who can better use the money, hand it over. But remember, if the person says he just needs gas money, he won't go to Arco; he'll go right back and buy into a small game, because all the down-and-outers think their luck has to change.

TIP 54

Do not pay attention to superstitions.

Here are some of the card superstitions I've encountered over the years:

1. When you have a run of bad cards, if you lay your handkerchief flat on the chair and sit on it, your luck will change.
2. If you turn your chair around three times or walk around it three times, your luck will improve.
3. The most unlucky card to hold is the 4 ♣.
4. It is very unlucky to sit with your legs crossed when playing cards.
5. Having a dog in the room while playing cards causes disputes.

If you have ever detoured to prevent a black cat from crossing your path, walked around a ladder rather than underneath it, broken a mirror and despaired over the next seven years, or canceled a flight scheduled for Friday the 13th, you have superstitious tendencies and may be the type of player who believes asking for a new deck will change your luck.

The most common superstition in cardrooms is that one chair is luckier than the next, because it's getting all the winning hands. People also believe that some dealers are poison, because they allegedly never deal a winning hand. One time I was playing in a game and Jose was sitting in the dealer's box, and every player (except me) claimed Jose was bad luck and got up to take a walk. I asked Jose, "Is it true you never deal a winning hand?" Of course you see the absurdity—Jose deals a winning hand to someone with each new shuffle of the deck. The money can't levitate off the table and deposit itself into Jose's checking account.

> "Particularly important . . . is to avoid putting on any article of clothing in which I have had a bad night in the past. Unfortunately, a too-strict observance of this rule always leads to a problem with shoes because I have only a limited number, and I've had terrible nights in every pair I own."
>
> —Edward Allen

SUPERSTITIONS LEAVE YOU VULNERABLE

Amateurs aren't the only silly kumquats at the table. I know one successful mid-limit player who laughed gleefully after I lost a tough hand. Safe to say we weren't the presidents of each other's fan clubs. He sat there with five racks of chips in front of him and an annoying grin of superiority. I pointed at his chips, made a crazy gesture with my hand, and said, "Whiffy boom bah bat gas, and may your chips be forever hexed!" Over the next few hours, rack after rack of his chips disappeared into other players' stacks. He became more and more agitated, playing worse and worse. I just nodded knowingly with a smug expression, as each pot was pushed in the opposite direction. When he was down to his last rack, he turned to me and yelled, "I will *never* play with you again! You have committed evil. You *never* put a hex on a Chinese man's chips; it's forbidden!" Is that a Buddhist precept I've never heard? If so, Buddha must have been hit on the head with an acorn when he came up with it. And why on earth would you ever tell someone your most dreaded superstition? If I were really nasty, I'd hex his damn chips each time I sat down with him. (And let me tell you, he's not a nice person, so it's hard to resist the live-short-and-don't-prosper whammy.)

Don't be a fool to randomness. As the lead vocalist of the New Main Street Singers said in the comedy *A Mighty Wind*, "Superstition is hooey, and you have to have a screw loose to believe in that stuff."

10
As Phony as a Back-Alley Prada Handbag

The Art of Bluffing—and How to Avoid Being Bluffed

TIP 55

Consider a bluff if everyone checked on the previous round.

The capability to bluff your opponents is the most sophisticated weapon in your gutsy-girl arsenal. Don't sell it to the Iraqis. Most players can conquer a table with an AK-47 (a pair of aces), but to be able to seek out and destroy the enemy by shooting marshmallows is creative poker.

A successful bluff involves choosing the right player(s) at the right time. The fewer players you need to snow, the better.

A successful bluff involves choosing the right player(s) at the right time. The fewer players you need to snow, the better. A poor strategy is attempting to bluff (or **semi-bluff***) too frequently, because players will catch on and fire chips back. Be

***Semi-bluff—the act of betting a hand that has the potential of becoming the best hand, but isn't at the time of the bet.**

selective. Target the thinkers or the perpetual folders—not the maniacs or the **calling stations*** who are always willing to pay to see.

Successful bluffing usually involves a plan that develops before the river card or that springs out of special circumstances. A spontaneous river bet made out of desperation that's inconsistent with the prior action is unlikely to work. If you hear a little voice in your brain saying, "If I don't bet, I can't win," heed it like an air-raid whistle—retreat and check. Before you attempt a bluff, review the betting patterns of the previous rounds and evaluate whether your opponent can assume you're holding a big enough hand for him to fold. If there's been no evidence, previous to the river, that you are, think twice.

Players with an erratic table image have a harder time bluffing, because they always get called. I'm that type, and I'm satisfied with making more money from my good hands than a player with a tight image would make with the same cards. The image of being a tight player is the best vantage point for making a bluff.

Bluffing isn't as frequent an occurrence as you might think in *limit* poker, because **pot odds**** usually dictate that a call be made. That's why it's often easier to bluff on the early streets when the pots are smaller. The more adept you are at card reading (knowing what your opponent may have), the more likely you will be to pull off a successful bluff.

*Calling station—**a passive player who regularly calls all bets, doesn't raise, and rarely folds.**

Pot odds—the ratio of the size of the pot compared to the size of the bet a player must call.**

The Dos of bluffing:

- **Do** bluff the player who just sat down. He won't be looking for snipers early in his session, and he'll be playing tightly.
- **Do** bluff any player who has just gotten even. He'll likely be so exhausted from struggling back from negative territory that he'll already have fallen asleep in the foxhole.
- **Do** bluff the sweet-talking enemy. If an opponent has shown interest in you outside of being a fellow poker player, take him prisoner.
- **Do** bluff the opponent who comments on how tight you play. Instead of being annoyed, be thankful or grateful for the great propaganda he's issuing on your behalf.
- **Do** attempt more bluffs when everyone has checked on the previous round and you're in last position. Watch your opponents carefully to determine whether they're waving white flags or preparing for an ambush.

The Don'ts of bluffing:

- **Don't** bluff someone who dislikes you. If he is emotionally invested in beating you, he'll never lay down his weapon.
- **Don't** bluff the short stack. He's already lost his arms and legs; he figures he has nothing left to lose and will call out of defeat.
- **Don't** bluff the maniac on a suicide mission.
- **Don't** bluff the same player twice if you failed the first time. If the enemy has discovered your game plan, he will suspect another strike. Wait for good cards before your next battle with him.
- **Don't** bluff if the table perception is that you're on tilt. The enemy knows that bluffing is always plan B if you're wide open and flailing.

- **Don't** bluff to advertise that you're a bad player. Some experts believe this will get you more action, but I think it'll just cost you more money.
- **Don't** bluff if your hand looks like an obvious draw. (For example, in stud a king raises, and you call with a 6♥. On fourth street the king catches a queen, and you catch the 5♥. When you call your opponent's bet, the hand he is most likely going to put you on is a flush draw with straightening possibilities. On the river your opponent will check with any hand less than a flush. Now is *not* the time to attempt a bluff, because the majority of players will automatically call.)

When You Suspect a Bluff

If you suspect that your opponent has very little, you cannot call with a pitiful hand and hope to win. You *must* raise!

The most extraordinary and ill-conceived bluff I ever made was in a $40/$80 hold 'em game, when I bet into a Mt. Everest pot almost for the hell of it. The experienced players were forlorn, knowing that there's no way I would attempt a bluff if I hadn't made my flush. They both folded. The amateur loon called. I sighed and turned over queen-high. My opponent jumped up, giggling and singing, "I knew she had nothing; I knew she had nothing!" I asked in disgust (at myself), "Whaddayagot?" He proudly turned over jack-high, which was as good as having one chopstick to move a beach. My example points out perfectly that you can be psychic and know your opponent is bluffing, but if your hand is so weak it can't stand up on its own, there is no other alternative but to raise or fold. (Note: I got away with bluffing a hand that should win only once in nine life times. Luckily for me, I'm a Cat.)

- **Don't** fall into the trap of believing everyone is trying to bluff you.

There is a way to punish the player who bluffs too much. For example, if you have a strong hand, such as aces, and are fairly sure your opponent will fold his hand if you bet, check and let him take a shot at bluffing you. Just be prepared to call when he bets. Bluffers are less likely to take a shot at you if you have been aggressive on the early rounds. When a new player you don't know sits down, don't be too quick to throw your hand away when he bets. It's best to establish up front that you won't be bullied by a bet or used for target practice. If it turns out that he's a conservative player, you can change your modus operandi and fold more selectively later.

TIP 56

A check-raise is more likely to be a straight-forward bet than a bluff.

A check-raise is designed to trap a player holding a weaker hand and is less likely to be a bluff than a straight-forward bet. If an opponent has a strong hand and is seeking to make an additional bet, he will check, hoping your hand is strong enough to bet; and if you do bet, he will smugly raise. Because a check-raise has a particular sting, many players will automatically throw in chips without thinking. A player check-raising understands this tendency and usually hopes to be called. That's why a check-raise is used sparingly to bluff an opponent out of a pot. If you are on the receiving end of a check-raise, always count to 10 and allow the sting to dissipate before you act. When you feel calm, take an additional few moments to evaluate with whom you're playing, how confident he appears, what his level of expertise is, whether he just won or lost the last hand, whether his past check-raises have been valid, and so on. Don't hurry your decision.

If you are on the receiving end of a check-raise, always count to 10 and allow the sting to dissipate before you act.

But if the same player—or any other player at the table—begins continually check-raising you, he may be taking advantage of your discipline in folding. There are two alternative actions: 1) Wait for a big hand that enables you to raise his check-raise, 2) check behind him periodically with a marginal hand, forcing him to miss a bet.

Check-raising is an overrated play, because often the player attempting to be wily misses a bet rather than gaining an additional one. If you are the check-raiser, be certain you are checking into a player who is aggressive enough to bet. Missed bets are expensive and also give your opponent a greater chance of drawing out on you for free.

When a player has check-raised successfully, he often thinks he has already won by outplaying you. Who are you to argue? Your medium hand is no good. Just fold.

TIP 57

Do not become obsessed with revenge if you are shown a bluff.

Your opponent raises pre-flop and you reraise with a pair of 10s. He calls. The flop is J♥ 2♣ 3♠. He checks. You bet. He calls. The turn is the 8♣. He checks. You bet. He calls. On the river a king pops up and your opponent bets. You think for a long time and decide that your opponent's starting hand could have been A-K. After a delay, you fold. He then shows A♣ 4♣. He bluffed you. He played for an inside straight or an ace on the flop, turned a flush draw, and took a shot at bluffing on the river. A reasonable play. But being shown the bluff makes you hotter than a Mexican chili pepper (especially because two other players guffawed).

The very next hand, the same opponent raises again, and you reraise him with J♠ 10♠. But the scenario is a little different; he reraises. The flop comes K♥ Q♠ 8♠. You have both a straight and a flush draw. He bets; you **pop it***; he reraises. You're so angry from the embarrassment of the last hand (and you still could be the favorite after all), you pop it again, and he raises again. Uh oh, you're in deep doo-doo. The turn is the 8♦. He bets and you call. The river is the ace you yearned for.

***Pop it—raise.**

When he bets, you're so delighted you can't put the raise in fast enough. He thinks for a nanosecond and reraises you. Only at this point do you even register what his holding is. Of course he could have a full house with kings, queens, or aces, but you don't care—you couldn't bear it if he showed another bluff, so you call. He shows you aces full of eights. You tilted plain and simple, and were punished to the maximum. Why did you "go off"? Because even pre-flop you became obsessed with outplaying him and pushed a hand way past its logical limit.

If you are shown a bluff and you can feel your blood start to boil, either get up and take a break or make certain the next hand you play against the offender is a superior one. He expects that you'll be exacting revenge, and is more likely to call with a medium-strength hand. If he's an expert player, he'll even reraise you with a marginal hand. Being shown a bluff gives you a sinking feeling. You'll probably tally the chips you lost and curse yourself for being duped. But the truth is, *all* good players get bluffed at one time or another. Sometimes a situation just lends itself to a bluff, because you have opponents behind you left to act. It happens. Let it go.

If you are shown a bluff and you can feel your blood start to boil, either get up and take a break or make certain the next hand you play against the offender is a superior one. He expects that you'll be exacting revenge, and is more likely to call with a medium-strength hand.

Once in a seven-card stud game my board showed four exposed hearts. I bet on the river and a solid player raised me. He knows I have a flush, I thought, and if he knows that, of course he can beat it. True? I folded and he showed that he'd missed his own flush and outplayed me by raising. Not many players are capable of folding a made flush, but he calculated correctly that I was. I can bring myself back to the feelings of that moment like it was yesterday, even though it was more than 17 years ago. If I hadn't moved from Las Vegas to California, I'd still be trying to get even with Tommy Fischer. So when I say, "Let it go," I admit it's a teacher saying, "Do as I say, not as I do." It injures the psyche and clutters the mind to not accept being outwitted. What good does it do me to hope no one remembers Tommy's next birthday? No good at all.

DON'T START SECOND GUESSING

Another residual effect of being shown a bluff is that suddenly you'll think the world is out to get you. You'll start to flounder, calling every future hand unnecessarily because you fear being embarrassed again. Know that the person who showed you the bluff is hoping you'll react in just this way. So be aware of a change in your attitude and fight your paranoia. For in fact, it's more likely your opponents won't try to bluff you from this point on, because they've all been there and can identify with the sudden onset of distrusting everyone.

Trying to exact revenge often leads to future disasters, because you're pushing a moment that no longer exists. The bluffer and the entire table are going to expect you to go on tilt. Don't live up to their expectations. Playing normally will more likely trick them than searching for ways to finesse the situation.

TIP 58

Showing a bluff is similar to throwing the first punch. Arm yourself.

Unless you are prepared for the dynamics of the game to change, do not show a bluff.

You like your opponents to be predictable, and if they have a score to settle, they won't be. In addition, you'll be dealing with a player who is angry at you, and it's much harder to play in an atmosphere of tension. On top of that, men and women sometimes gang up on the opposite sex. Tom, the player you bluffed, is now a worry, but unknown to you, Moe, Larry, and Curly have joined the effort to right the wrong against their brother. Why put yourself voluntarily in front of a firing squad?

If your bluff fails, there are measures you can take to prevent your opponent from realizing your intention was robbery. Even though he won the hand, you still don't want him to know you bluffed because he may try to repay the favor with a little thievery of his own. Try to trick him by asking what he has before turning over your hand. His reaction may be to turn his hand over first, and you'll be saved from revealing yours. If he shows the winner, muck your cards quickly (making certain they can't be retrieved from the discard pile). Whatever he had, say you had something

> **Stone-Cold Bluffs Can Be Hot Plays**
>
> A bluff doesn't have to work all of the time to make it a good play. For example, if you bet $30 to win a $300 pot, you need to win only slightly more than 10 percent of the time to make a profit. In fact, if you win most of your bluffs, you're not bluffing often enough. There's absolutely no shame in getting caught in a bluff, because it's an essential part of any good poker player's game.

reasonable too. As goofy and unbelievable as this may sound, sometimes when I'm caught in a bluff, I put this startled look on my face and say, "What a dunce cap. I misread my hand." There's a tiny chance someone will believe it, so it's worth the misrepresentation—no, let's face it, lie.

TIP 59

If you have a great hand on the river and get raised, call rather than fold.

A few times I've been bluffed because I overestimated my opponent's ability to read my hand. What looked like an obvious flush to me looked like only two pair to him. What looked like an obvious set of trips on fourth street to me, looked like only sixes to him. I believed he knew the strength of my hand and, therefore, he must have a better one, so I folded incorrectly.

The time you are most likely to be bluffed is when everything about your opponent's body language convinces you he has the best hand. Why is the bluff so convincing? Because he actually believes it too. This is likely to happen when you have high respect for the raiser because of his reputation as the poker-room pro. The best of the best sometimes misjudge a situation too. The few times I've folded winning hands, such as trips, straights, or flushes, it was because I was overly impressed by an opponent's reputation. And because he thought he had the best hand, I believed him.

> "If you are never caught bluffing, you are either the best bluffer in the history of poker or you are not bluffing enough. If you are caught almost every time you bluff, you're bluffing much too frequently."
>
> —Richard Harroch and Lou Krieger *Poker for Dummies*

There are just too many hands you can beat with a big hand. Your opponent may be misreading your strength or pushing a medium-strong hand. Your hand doesn't have to be a monster to be the winner. Often you have the correct pot odds for a call, no matter how much it looks like you are beat. Allow me to reiterate: If you think you have a great hand on the river, don't be a fallen hero and fold when you get raised.

11

How to Keep All Your Balls in the Air Without Getting Hit on the Head

Staying Balanced When Things Go Wrong

TIP 60

You're never as good as you think you are when you're winning, or as bad as you think you are when you're losing.

Wow! What a day—$2,500 worth of winnings! No one can knock you off your mountain of chips. Yes, indeed, the queen rules! There's only one other player winning at the table, Joking Johnny, and even he doesn't look happy. Ha! Normally Johnny raises every one of your bets, but not today. Maybe it's time to give him a little needle.

Tsk, tsk, Your Highness, did you happen to forget the inside straight you made in the $1,000 pot against Johnny's three kings? A little lucky, don't you think? Oh, I see, that was pure skill.

Often when we win, we peer down at the plebeians and think, I'm up here in my chip castle because I'm so good, and you're down there in the alligator moat because you're so common. Winners are satisfied with being winners and are less apt to admit—or even to think about—errors or to recognize plain dumb luck. I don't want to rain on your royal parade, but just because you have all the chips doesn't mean you outplayed your opponents. Luck may have played a greater component than skill. Be careful. You just may find yourself getting dethroned, unless you are as critical of your play when you're winning as when you are losing.

Often when we win, we peer down at the plebeians and think, I'm up here in my chip castle because I'm so good, and you're down there in the alligator moat because you're so common.

Let's look through the mirror from the other side. What if you've been at the mercy of a specific player (we'll call him "the king" for the sake of the metaphor) during your past few sessions? Don't dutifully pledge the king your chips because you are resigned to losing. Snap out of it, queenie. Just because you've lost for a few days (even weeks) doesn't mean you should be submissive to His Highness' skill or that you're an inferior player. If short-term results easily topple your belief in yourself, you can become the victim of your own prophecy of doom. The pessimist always finds a way—if you expect to lose, you will.

Sometimes we lose because we played atrociously; sometimes we lose even when we did everything exactly right. It's up to you to be objective about which is which, because no one is going to look over your shoulder and provide you with a report card. Losing inevitably erodes your confidence, but you can't let yourself relinquish your perspective or rely solely on results to judge your performance. Many professionals with healthy egos have faced the crossroad of loss of confidence. All you can do during a losing streak is to continue to play your best game and wait for the cards to turn in your favor.

TIP 61

If you are not prepared to lose the next set of trips with composure, go home!

Here's the scenario: You've been bludgeoned with a few bad beats, and then you get dealt a **rolled-up hand*** against a table of clowns. You're thrilled, but anxious—could life be so cruel as to deal you a 425-to-1 shot and crush you again? Your nerves are jangled, and you become so emotionally involved in the outcome of the hand that you promise yourself, If I lose this, I'll never play poker again. Girlfriend, if you are looking for justice in the outcome of your hands, you shouldn't be playing. Cards have no memory—they are little rectangles of plastic-coated cardboard with spots on them. Why on earth would you believe

***Rolled-up hand—in seven-card stud when the first three cards dealt are of the same rank (ex. 9-9/9).**

they'd understand the concept of fair or unfair? There isn't any difference between a playing card and a Ken doll. Neither of them knows anything.

There isn't any difference between a playing card and a Ken doll. Neither of them knows anything.

You've got to remember that the last three hands you lost are completely independent of the next one you'll play. Here's a way to test your frame of mind before you ante up for the next deal. Imagine yourself being dealt a pocket pair of aces against three opponents, all with a nine door card. Now imagine yourself losing to a **wheel***. If just the thought makes you mumble any word associated with homicide, it's time to clock out for the day.

TIP 62

Do not take the cards personally.

We all wish there were a simple reason for why we lose, but it's not because we cursed at the sales clerk, stepped on a ladybug, or forgot our sister's birthday. The draw of the card that causes us to either win or lose a hand is completely random. However, if you put

*Wheel—**A-2-3-4-5 (also called a bicycle).**

yourself at a statistical **advantage***, you will win in the long run. Don't dwell on the things you can't control. Instead, concentrate on the things you can, such as playing good cards, keeping your emotions under control, and staying focused and in the present. This is not easy to do, but work on it—it's important.

Just as we shouldn't take the weather personally, we shouldn't take what cards we are dealt personally either. Whether we are dealt sunshine or hail stones, the key is to maintain equanimity with poise, integrity, and self-respect. Just as in life, our actions and reactions are the only things we can truly own.

TIP 63

Be more conservative when you're losing.

One reason we play poker is for the stimulation of being involved in the action of a hand. But, on average, in a full game we muck our cards 90 percent of the time and become spectators to others having fun. This is tolerable when we are winning, but when we're losing, we get itchy to return to that feeling of well-being associated with winning. Hands we normally would discard as inferior, such as small

***Advantage**—the edge a good player has in a poker game due to skill versus luck.**

pairs and ace-**baby***, take on a new appealing glow. Our focus switches from making money to promising the Lord 20 percent if He'll just give us two face cards. The deeper we dig into our wallets, the more yummy a pair of fours in first position starts to look. But the yummy one, from the perspective of your opponents, is you. As you start playing worse, you're going to look as juicy as a pork chop to a Rottweiler.

YOU DON'T HAVE TO GIVE ACTION TO GET ACTION

After you've taken a bad beat, make the next hand you play a quality choice. Your normally aggressive game of raising with marginal hands will only encourage your opponents to become more assertive. You may as well burn your money if you try a bluff—that's what your opponent is expecting.

What can you do when players think your raises are meaningless? Simple. Throw a curveball. Instead of being overly aggressive, become overly passive with a good hand and let your opponents think you have nothing. You've given them an opportunity to misjudge a situation and to bet your hand for you or even attempt a bluff. Now you've turned yourself into an unpredictable player, and it'll be very confusing to them at the **showdown**** because they expected you to keep throwing fastballs. When your stack begins to build again, you can turn back into the table intimidator.

*Baby—**a small card; for example, a deuce, trey, four, five, or six.**

Showdown—after all the betting is done, the opponents turn up their hands to determine the winner.**

TIP 64

Do not educate your opponents out of sympathy or for any other reason.

Losing is always a bummer, even more so when you are sitting with a group of cartoon characters who don't know odd from even, and sometimes it's hard not to act like a sore sport. Out of misplaced pride, you may want to demonstrate that you're not a loser and know more about poker than Doyle Brunson has learned in his many decades of being top banana. Well, go holler it in a bomb shelter. No one needs to hear you give the odds on making a flush with one card to come, expound on when to try a semi-bluff, or brag about how much you won last year. It makes you look foolish, may actually educate a weaker player, and proves that you don't know as much about the game as you thought or you wouldn't be indulging an ego-based flaw.

Betty, a feisty player, began her poker career with an incredible talent for reading cards, but she was weak in mathematical elements of the game. For example, she'd often incorrectly raise out players from an early position on a flush draw. A single such flaw can be very costly, and it's a long-term moneymaker for an opponent holding a high pair, because she protects his hand by clearing the field and playing heads up with him.

But Betty is a smart cookie, and she had to be told only once that she was a numbskull by a pissed-off player holding the high pair when she made her flush. He was obliging enough to tell her exactly why her skull was numb, and he corrected a major error in her game in a 60-second spew. Why did the loser feel compelled to educate her? Because if he couldn't be rewarded with justice, he could get some type of satisfaction announcing she was clueless. Betty wasn't embarrassed; she was wisely appreciative of new information that would improve her game and continued to stack his chips. That was 20 years ago, now when she sits down, she's a force to contend with. Recently, after she beat one of the guys who used to berate her, I heard her say, "Thanks, Marty, for all your past advice. Now when I kick your ass, you have no one to blame but yourself."

ALL'S FAIR IN LOVE AND WAR

Another mistake to avoid is educating a player you're sweet on. What happens when the romance ends and you've given away your secrets? Your former honey outplays you, that's what! I continually make the mistake of trying to impress NBA stars at the table, because I fall under the spell of their notoriety. When they do flirt with me, I'm so damn grateful that I return the favor by whispering stuff like, "You're getting too aggressive, wait for a hand, don't bluff so much . . ." Here I am giving advice to guys who are competitive lions with huge bankrolls, and the only advantage I have is the information I hold that they don't. Is that a fair

> Do as I say, not as I do—don't fall in crush with a player who has a twinkle in his eye and a lot of poker potential.

exchange for a comment such as, "Great haircut, Cat"? If Tony Parker sat down, I'd probably hand-deliver him an instructional manual and offer to give private lessons. Once again, do as I say, not as I do—don't fall in crush with a player who has a twinkle in his eye and a lot of poker potential.

PUT YOUR SYMPATHY ASIDE

Because women are the more empathic gender, they are vulnerable to feeling sorry for an opponent. Don't let your sympathy cost you money. Players sit down at the table of their own free will. Don't tell a player that he's playing over his head, he should go home, he's on tilt, or he has a gambling problem. I once suggested to a poker acquaintance that it wasn't the best idea to play high stakes after a breakup. He told me women aren't to be trusted and to mind my own business. I watched him lose $9,000 in two hours. I felt terrible for him.

Many times you'll watch someone lose money and it'll break your heart, but you can't afford to be a social worker or an amateur therapist at the table. Once a sweet lost soul told me, "My wife said if I come home broke tonight, she's leaving me." I looked down at the sixty bucks left in front of him and said: "If I don't win this, somebody else will. Sorry, but I'm going to raise you all in." I gave him twenty bucks for gas when he left the table, and he went to a smaller game and bought in again with the money.

DON'T TELL THE TELL

Another commandment: Never cut off your cash cow by revealing a player's tell. Ten years ago there was a very rich player at the Mirage named Mr. Ed, who was juicy enough to drag players out of bed with the midnight rumor that he had trotted into the poker room. With 100-percent consistency, if he had a flush draw, he would say he had a big pair. If he had a big pair, he'd say he was playing a draw. It wasn't a subtle tell—even the weekend tourist would pick up on the fact that Mr. Ed was a hopelessly bad liar. It was such a big advantage to keep him talking, especially since he played nine hands out of 10, that he may as well have been playing with his cards face up.

One night an insecure, hot-tempered fellow from Chicago, nicknamed the "Clubber," became so frustrated when he couldn't beat Mr. Ed that he yelled, "You're so ignorant, Ed, and everyone knows that if you say you have aces you don't have a pair!" It may have made the Clubber feel superior for a moment, but his big mouth caught up with him the very next hand when Mr. Ed reversed his tell and **trapped*** Chicago Club. Not only did the goofball ruin his own chances for predicting Mr. Ed's holdings, but he became very unpopular with the rest of the pros who had been profiting for months from the tell.

Remember that tells are rare and extremely valuable. If someone reveals one of your own to you, don't be annoyed. Be grateful—he's just saved you money.

***Trapping—playing in such a way as not to let your opponent know you have a big hand, thus inducing him to bluff or to bet a weaker hand.**

12

The Right Shoes Can Make All the Difference (Just Ask Cinderella)

Advanced Techniques to Increase Your Win Rate

TIP 65

Use every opportunity that comes your way to brag about how lucky you are.

Any theorist who claims there is no such thing as luck is dead wrong! If you get hit by an airplane falling from the sky, that would be pretty damn unlucky. If you discover that you are a long-lost heir to Aristotle Onassis, that would be lucky. What you can't do is predict luck.

I have a friend who constantly bemoans his bad luck. I've pointed out to him that he was born in the United States, not Afghanistan or Sudan. That's lucky. He was born with a 160 IQ. That's lucky too. He wasn't born looking like the elephant man—in fact, he's kind of cute. That's pretty lucky. He has plenty of money, and not all of it came from working long hours in the mines. That's certainly not unlucky. He was born male. Is that lucky? I'd say so. Considering all these factors, I think he's probably in the top 3 percent of the luckiest people in the world. But there's no changing his mind—he doesn't want to know where the light switch is. If he were a poker player and made a full house, he'd complain that he got only four callers to pay it off instead of five. He doesn't understand that if you choose to look at the sunny side of the street instead of the side in shadow, your luck actually increases because at least you're happier.

> "'If I live long enough the luck will change. I have had bad luck now for fifteen years. If I ever get any good luck, I will be rich.' He grinned. 'I am a really good gambler, really I would enjoy being rich.'
>
> 'Do you have bad luck with all games?'
>
> 'With everything and with women.' He smiled again, showing his bad teeth."
>
> —Ernest Hemingway
> "The Gambler, the Nun, the Radio"

IN THE SHORT RUN, LUCK PLAYS A BIGGER ROLE

You'll hear many a player whine, "When are the cards going to break even?" What they mean is, when am I going to be dealt my fair share of good hands. One friend, who is a high-limit player and mathematician, told me, "If I knew then what I know now about the short run versus the long run in poker, I'd never have started playing." The long run is *much* longer than most educated poker players would expect. Do the cards break even in a lifetime? They may; they may not. It's daunting, isn't it? But don't let this dampen your enthusiasm for the game. If you are a good player, there is only a small chance that you will be a lifetime loser.

The poker room is a place where being perceived as lucky *is* lucky. I want everyone I play with to think that, second to Dolly Parton, I'm the luckiest girl in the whole USA. If I draw out in a hand and hear gripes, I'll quip, "What can I say—I'm lucky." Any opportunity you have to brag about your good luck helps to foster the illusion that somehow you have magical powers. The superstitious players will believe you, and the sensible players who know your bologna has a first name will still have trouble controlling their envy.

The poker room is a place where being perceived as lucky *is* lucky.

TIP 66

Deceptive play is most effective against analytical players. (Or, don't try to trick the dummies.)

Let's start with an example of a deceptive play. In stud, when everyone has folded to the low card, it's normal to raise as the last person to act. If the player with the low card is a thoughtful player, he'll expect the raise. But what if I don't raise? Let's say I simply call with a high card showing and junk in the **pocket***. He's going to be suspi-

***Pocket—the downcards.**

cious. If I catch another high card on fourth street and bet, his suspicion may lead him to fold more readily than if I'd initially raised*. But if I make the same play against a player who thinks one-dimensionally, he'll believe I didn't raise because I have nothing and be more likely to call on fourth street, regardless of what card I catch.

Let's look at a second example of deceptive play, this time in hold 'em. You're in a three-way pot on the river. In first position is player A, the thinker; you're player B, the genius in middle position; player C is the novice in last position. A third suited card hits the river. The thinker, who was the aggressor on all streets, takes notice of the heart but bets anyway. You contemplate. Has your play on all betting rounds been consistent with being on a flush draw? If you raise with a total bust, you need to get two players to fold. You know player A (the strong player) is capable of folding for a raise, because you've seen him do so in previous hands. Regardless of his bet, you know he fears you made a flush, and if you didn't, he's hoping to extract an additional bet from the novice. The question is, will it dawn on the amateur that player A must have a strong hand to bet, and you must have a monster hand to raise? Rely on the body language of the novice to swing your vote. If his attention is rapt, pass on the bluff. But if he is fidgeting or looking away from the action, go for it.

This example shows how many layers there are to consider and why a good recall of how hands were played earlier in the game assists in making more accurate decisions—in this case about your chances for a successful

***I recommend using this play only occasionally.**

bluff. Keep in mind that this isn't a chess game—you don't have lots of time to consider all the possibilities. In general, players expect you to react within 30 seconds or less. But if you take more time, don't worry that you'll necessarily be giving away the strength of your hand. A professional won't regard a measured pause as lack of confidence, because you could be **Hollywooding***.

Poker isn't chess—you don't have lots of time to consider all the possibilities. In general, players expect you to react within 30 seconds or less.

Some players are brilliant at taking advantage of a three-way bluffing situation, because they are excellent card readers and have weighed the skill level of each player long before the hand arrived. One of my proudest moments was bluffing two skilled players. I had the advantage of acting last, and the flop came 7-3-3. The first player bet out, the second player raised, and I just called the bet with zippo. Both players' radars were activated. What could I have? On the turn, the first player checked, the second player cautiously bet, and I raised with a stone-cold bluff. Both players fired their hands into the muck, because what else could I have but a trey or two sevens? In this instance my advanced play worked, because I was matching wits with two thinkers who possessed self-control, and they knew I wasn't a lunatic.

When you have an itch to be tricky, always pick on the experienced player versus the novice. The weak player won't understand what the bet means, while the analytical player will be vulnerable to falling into your web of deceit.

*Hollywooding—**hamming it up in an amateurish way to attempt deception.**

TIP 67

Do not try to discourage a bet if you intend to call.

I see lots of players trying to discourage their opponents from betting by readying chips in their hands, essentially telling the potential bettor, "If you bet, it's one hundred percent I'm going to call." Let's say you're the bettor and observe this behavior. Why would you attempt a bluff if your opponent has as much as said, "You bet, and I'm calling?"

If you intend to call a bet, it's not wise to hold chips over the pot as a threat. You *want* to give your opponent the chance to bluff. If you plan to call anyway, it's free money. If you signal your intention to call, you're not discouraging your opponent to bet if he has a good hand; you're discouraging a bet only if he doesn't, which is the opposite of what you're hoping for.

TIP 68

Keep records of your plays.

Has someone ever told you a poker story but forgotten key aspects of the play? It's maddening to listen intently, then suddenly the storyteller doesn't remember a critical component of the hand, such as what position he was in, or whether it was a single or double raise he had to fade. Even worse is when the cards change during the tale. First he says an eight hit the turn, and I point out that an eight would have given him a straight. Then he says, "No, no, now I remember. It was a jack." Egad! How can you analyze a hand after the fact if you can't even remember the cards?

I counter my risky urges by forcing myself to patiently wait a round before anteing or blinding. This enables me to study the climate from a spectator's clearheaded point of view and to get centered before risking any money.

In case you're wondering, excellent players have little trouble remembering the hands they've played, even as long as a week ago (the exceptional hands will be remembered forever). If you're shaking your head in disbelief, take notes to practice your recall. As soon as a hand is completed, surreptitiously jot down in shorthand the exact sequence of cards and the detailed play. If a hand puzzles you, or if you commit an error, make a note—even take notes on hands that you think you played brilliantly. After the session is over, transcribe your shorthand into a poker journal and study all the aspects of how the hand played out. Maybe your error originated in your choice of a starting hand, perhaps you were overly aggressive with an ace and weak **kicker***, or maybe you called too many bets on the river, and so forth. Within a short time, you will be able to identify your weaknesses and consider ways to prevent costly boo-boos from reoccurring.

***Kicker—the highest unpaired card that helps determine the value of a five-card poker hand.**

It's also helpful to record situations in which your emotions caused an embarrassing belly flop or, worse, made you jump aboard a runaway train. It's not usually the loss of one hand that causes us to tilt, but rather a combination of events: Hand No. 1, you have trips and lose to a flush. Hand No. 2, you fail to make your flush draw against the same player, who wins with deuces. Hand No. 3, you start with inferior cards because you're experiencing mind warp, and you lose because justice never seems to give you a break. Think about all this after the fact, and analyze why the wreck occurred and how you could have avoided it.

My particular bugaboo is jumping off to a bad start by gambling too much. Psychologically, it is safer for me to wait for a strong hand to begin my session rather than risk having second pair and virtually **drawing dead***. I counter my risky urges by forcing myself to patiently wait a round before anteing or blinding. This enables me to study the climate from a spectator's clearheaded point of view and to get centered before risking any money. I identified this weakness through my notes and figured out how to rein in my chomping-at-the-bit eagerness to feel the rush of action.

I know that the likelihood of you actually carrying through with this suggestion is less than, what, 20 percent? But if you truly want to play poker well, it involves putting in more effort than just playing. Athletes put in a lot more time practicing for a game than they do in the game itself. Playing the game is the payoff for all the hard work that came before. It's not just the hours you spend at the table that count, but also the time you put in reviewing your own

*Drawing dead—**when no card left in the deck will give you a winning hand.**

game tapes, reading books, and actively thinking about how to become a better player even when you're on the bench.

TIP 69

There are advantages to being on the right or left of an expert player or a maniac.

What do sex and poker have in common? They both are arts that require a mastery of positions. I don't think there's a right or wrong answer as to whether the top or bottom is preferable in sex, or whether it's better to be on the left or right in poker, but I am willing to tell you my right and left preferences. Personally, I like acting first against the expert, so I prefer to be on his right. This means he is forced to react to me, rather than the other way around.

What do sex and poker have in common? They both are arts that require a mastery of positions.

Most players want to sit on an expert's left, because it's more comfortable to be the raiser than the raised. I feel this way about being raised: It's not the worst thing that will ever happen to me. If I don't have a good hand, I fold; if I have a sweet one, I raise back. It's not as if I'm going to be dragged out in the courtyard at sunrise and shot if I raise and get reraised back. If I'm playing against an aggressive player, I can steal more pots because I'll be acting first. It's like being the first one to pull out a gun. If you prefer to be passive in relation to the expert, I can understand how snuggling in on his left is cozier for you. That allows you to choose your spots to reraise him when you have a good hand.

POSITION AND THE MANIAC

Whether it's better to sit to the right or left of a wild player is also a matter of how comfortable you are with being the aggressor. If you're seated to the maniac's left, it's a wild ride to continually isolate his poor hands with only marginal ones yourself. You'll have a big advantage by doing so, until the other players catch on and get mad as hell and **come over the top***. Once this happens regularly, shift into low gear and wait for bigger value hands. My recommendation is, don't be a Miss Piggy. Raise more than your share, but don't be so blatant that the other players become porkers themselves.

> Most players want to sit on an expert's left, because it's more comfortable to be the raiser than the raised.

But if you get stuck being on the maniac's right, there are still positive aspects. The maniac will be clearing the field for you by his relentless raising. You can simply limp with a hand of strength, let the maniac take control, see how the field reacts, and get a big advantage from being able to act from the button position (the sexiest of all). You may find yourself calling four bets

*Come over the top—**to reraise the raiser.**

with a pair of queens, or folding A-Q or a pair of 10s in last position (the right of a maniac), but when you do have the goods, your pots are going to be enormous.

The bottom line is that all positions, in sex and poker, have their advantages and disadvantages. If you just do what feels best, you'll probably find your natural side.

TIP 70

If you pause before acting on an obvious hand, it will look more natural when you linger over a hand that requires real thought.

A friend advised me, "When you're writing even the most basic tips, don't say, 'Of course this is obvious,' because sometimes even the most obvious things can be revelations." I'll bet that once you think about this tip, you'll murmur, "Well, that's obvious. I should have thought of that."

Calling with a flush draw that you know will win if completed is almost automatic, and you'll likely do it quickly without thinking. But don't! Pause. Allow your opponents to think you have something to ponder, and they may be deceived by your hesitation. You don't want to let the cat out of the bag when you actually do have something to deliberate, because it can reveal the strength of your hand. It's impossible to take the exact amount of time before you act with each decision, but if you sometimes appear thoughtful when you're not, your opponents won't be able to decipher the significance of a time delay in your overall play.

You don't want to let the cat out of the bag when you actually do have something to deliberate, because it can reveal the strength of your hand.

TIP 71

Don't tangle with the tilter when you hold a weak hand.

When a player is emotionally out of control—on tilt—he'll flail his arms in the deep end, silently screaming, "Help me, help me. I need to win chips *now*!" As brutal as it sounds, if someone is drowning in his own desperation, you're not obligated to pull him safely back to shore. That is the nature of poker. If you are going to get all drippy with sympathy, you aren't competitively tough enough to beat the game. Think of it this way: If it were a him-or-you situation, he'd be sailing off on the life raft without you.

One mistake good players make is to give the drowning man a lifeline by gambling with a weak hand. For example, say you're playing stud and the sinker raises again, this time with a 10 door card and a 10 out. You have sevens with a deuce kicker and a deuce out. Murky at best. Do you think just because he's on tilt that he'll never get a pair again? Even if you hold three cards higher than a seven, he can easily outdraw you. Throw the small ones back and try catching a bigger hand. His spirit is not going to be revived by winning the antes. Keep playing quality hands, just as you would if he weren't drowning. If you see him bobbing to the surface, hit him with a paddle!

TIP 72

Mix up your play occasionally, but don't use this as an excuse to play poorly.

Beginning players try to rationalize playing poor hands by using the excuse, "I was mixing up my play." If you just played a pair of fours for a double raise, you're not mixing up your play. You just stink—you fish! Mixing up your play does not mean giving up your advantage; it means playing the advantage in various ways. For example, the correct and normal play with aces is to raise. You do so 10 times, but the 11th time you decide to limp with aces to mix up your game. That's cool; it can trip up the observant player and definitely adds an element of uncertainty to your game. But you have to mix it up only once in a blue moon to keep that impression prickling in your opponents' minds. And if you mix it up against people who are as aware as corkscrews, you may have lessened your chances of winning for no reason at all.

Mixing up your play does not mean giving up your advantage.

TIP 73

Don't build up your opponent's confidence.

Flatterers drive me crazy! Not when they are praising me, but when they are praising my opponents. Resist inflating your opponent's ego by bringing up a recent tournament he won, or how well he played a hand, or how sickeningly superior he is as a player. Even the comment "Good call" coming from a player who failed to execute a bluff is a compliment that will puff your opponent's ego and raise his standard of play. You won't get any additional respect from a good player because you drool on him, and it'll just make him harder to beat. An ego boost gives *any* player an edge, because now he has a strong reason to try to live up to his reputation by playing great poker.

Poker Players as Celebrities

Many tournament poker players have become as popular as Hollywood movie stars. There is a rumor that Ben Affleck was standing next to WPT superstar Gus Hanson, and an autograph hound bypassed Ben to seek a souvenir signature from Gus. My advice is, keep your adulation to yourself. These guys don't need any more confidence than they already have. I don't care if you have a 12-inch by 24-inch glossy hanging over your bed of Phil Hellmuth, the "Poker Brat." If you are matched up with him in a game, play it cool. (Besides, he's married.)

TIP 74

Press those sessions when you are winning big.

Many amateur players want to quit when they are winning big—they hope to exit the game at a high point. My question is, how can you be sure where your high point is or when it's going to shift into reverse? If you are up $3,000 in a $20/$40 game, you are sailing, sister! Now you have an opportunity to own your table, steal more blinds, bluff, and make your opponents fear any raise and back off. Plus, it feels grand to play when your chips are skyscrapers compared to your opponents' one-story shacks. Why wouldn't you want to continue playing and take advantage of your dominating image? Just because you've never reached a peak of $3,000 before doesn't mean that today's session couldn't reach $5,000. Players have won that much in a $20/$40 game, but they usually haven't done so in a four-hour session. You need to put in the time. Be more prone to quit when you're a loser rather than a winner, a pattern of behavior not many pros possess. Any time you're capable of mastering an action that a better player can't, you're one step closer to becoming the better player.

My mentor, David Heyden, had one session at the Bicycle Club in which he won $34,000 in a $75/$150 stud game. He played from noon one day to noon the next. (That win translated into a $15/$30 profit would be $6,800.) How did he know when to stop? When he physically felt his mind getting wavy and the spots on the cards were blurring. True champions never relent and give their opponents a break, nor do they quit because they're scared of losing some of their profit back.

Just because you've never reached a peak of $3,000 before doesn't mean that today's session couldn't reach $5,000.

That said, I'm still an advocate of doing what's comfortable for you. The worst feeling in the world is to win, win, win, and be absolutely sure that you'll quit a winner, and then—bam!—a series of bad beats cripples your stack and you're reaching for your wallet. Crummy, crummy feeling. I'd rather lose straight out than be a big winner and have to go home a loser.

I have developed a method of avoiding that scenario by following this rule: If I've played more than five hours and have been winning easily, then suddenly see my fortune slipping away, I stop when I've lost 75 percent of my profit. I don't mean if I'm up a small amount. I'm talking about those times when chips start falling from the sky like snowflakes in Las Vegas—and then melt away just as rapidly.

I think it's critical to your pregame attitude to have quit a winner the previous day. You'll sit down to your new session feeling more powerful than if you'd lost the day before. That doesn't mean to play an hour, then quit when you're up $25 to preserve your streak. But if you've won 15 days in a row, it's close to quitting time, and you're on the teeter-totter of going home either a winner or a loser, quit now!

To Quit or Not to Quit?

Some experts pontificate that poker is just one long playing session, and you should be psychologically immune to your chip position. They believe if the game is good and you still have an advantage, you should keep playing. I challenge that assertion. It's theoretically correct, but it applies only to those rare players who can separate emotion from poker. Even after all these years, that's not me. Is it you?

13

Pssst, Do You Want to Know a Secret? Promise Not to Tell?

Insights the Pros Keep Under Their Hats

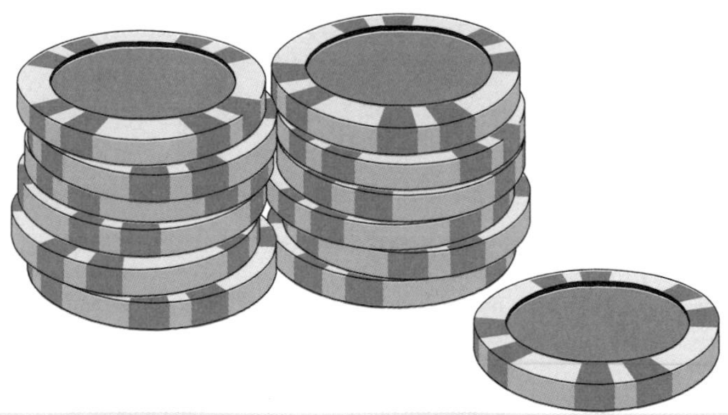

TIP 75

You're not at the table to make friends.

Live poker is a social game, and you can easily be distracted from your main reason for playing—which is to make money. Witty, lively players can be amusing, and suddenly you may find yourself caught up in the entertainment, wanting the jocularity to continue. You fear that if you check-raise the comedian, you might dampen the spirit of the table, so you **play soft*** and miss a bet. But that bet may represent an hour's worth of equity. Suddenly the ticket price is getting expensive. Don't hold back because you don't want to ruin the fun mood, or because a particular opponent tickles your fancy pants and you want to keep things friendly.

Don't hold back because you don't want to ruin the fun mood, or because a particular opponent tickles your fancy pants and you want to keep things friendly.

***Playing soft**—means not applying pressure by raising or bluffing.

Unless you're playing for very small stakes or you're Bill Gates, too much money is at risk to use poker solely as a social outlet. If you want to make friends, take a cooking class, go to Starbucks, or join a basketball league. If your purpose is to find a mate, try online dating. (I know from experience, poker players aren't the most desirable mates anyway. The worthwhile ones have trained themselves to feel as little emotion as possible; you may as well fall for Robby the Robot.)

YOU DON'T WANT TO BE MISS POPULARITY

On a different note, be suspicious if everyone is being unusually nice to you—even if you look like Miss Alabama. A good poker player's primary motive is to win your money, not to make a new friend. Even if he's been chatting you up all evening, when you're broke, you'll hear the tired old lie, "I'll call you," and he'll go back to peeking at his hole cards instead of your cleavage. The adage is true: If you look around and you don't see the sucker, it's probably you.

Surrounded by Admirers

Women at the table who are perceived as loaded are particularly prone to having attention lavished on them. If you are a woman with weak skills and lots of money, believe me, your newfound friends are fickle. Don't be susceptible to flattery. I'd rather have players snarling at me than cozying up to me, because that would mean I was viewed as a threat and a winner. When you are getting tons of attention, be honest with yourself as to what the reasons might be.

TIP 76

Do not fall in love with your hand.

Tick, tock, tick, tock—you've been waiting for a solid starting hand as long as you've been waiting for Mr. Right. Finally you take a peek and, voilà, there are those beautiful royal gentlemen—two red kings. You fall in love at first sight. Your heart pitter-patters as you raise and get two callers. Groan—the flop is 10-9-8 , all spades. The big blind bets out, and a middle-position player raises forcefully. Judas Priest, what do you do? Your options are to fold (curses), call (sigh), or raise (because when you said your vows, it meant forever).

In this situation there's as much to think about as when you're choosing your wedding dress. How does your hand measure up against that of an opponent who may be betting or raising on the come? And there's always the possibility of a flopped two pair, because 8-9 and 9-10 suited are connecting cards that appeal to some players as starting hands. You can't rule out that the bettor or the raiser didn't flop trips. The most disastrous scenario is that someone has already flopped a straight or a flush. Whatever has occurred, your kings are starving for attention. If a flop card pairs on the turn, it may give one of your opponents a full house. If any spade turns, or any straight card such as a seven or a jack, you're left at the altar. You reraise because—gosh darn it—you stand by your

cowboys*, and maybe the big blind will fold for two bets. Wishful thinking—he calls like it's a no-brainer. Uh oh, Ollie.

The turn card is the ace of clubs. The big blind checks. The original raiser bets. Even though you love your kings dearly, there are no excuses left to stay in this hand. The bettor easily could have made aces and 10s. The big blind (who checked) still may have a better hand than yours and trap you with a check-raise. It's one of poker's little disappointments: No matter how handsome a starting hand is, it can turn into a mismatched affair on the flop. You just can't afford to promise your love to the river.

TIP 77

Don't fall into the trap of making an assumption about an opponent's hand and never wavering from it.

Reading hands requires a mental balancing act—considering a variety of possibilities at the beginning and filtering down to a logical few as the hand proceeds. For

*Cowboy—**nickname for a king.**

example, let's say you're playing seven-card stud. You raise with queens, and your opponent calls with a 9♠. He's a tight player, and another nine is open on the table. So what are the possibilities? It is *highly* unlikely he actually has a pair of nines (unless he thinks you are bluffing and has an ace as a backup overcard). But if two or fewer spades are on board, he may have a three-flush with an ace or a king kicker. Or he may be slow-playing a pair higher than queens. Or he may be slightly tilting and have a pair lower than nines in the pocket, or he may have your pair—queens. See all the possibilities to consider?

On fourth street you catch a nine, and your opponent catches an offsuit ace. He checks and you bet with trepidation, because you're becoming suspicious of the rascal. He calls. It's safe to eliminate a pair of nines, because he's a tight player and would dump his hand. On fifth street he catches a 2♠ and checks. You bet, wishing that deuce had been red, and he pops it.

The possibilities are:

1. He started with an ace-high three-flush, caught another ace on fourth street, and waited until the expensive street to set a trap for more money.
2. He has buried aces in the pocket and made three aces.
3. He has buried deuces and made three ducks—unlikely, because he doesn't play that poorly.
4. He has a buried pair of kings.
5. He is raising on the come with a four-flush.
6. He's bluffing.

Considering all the possibilities in this situation, it appears that folding is the logical action. The least of all worries is a four-flush, and even then you're only a tiny favorite.

This example illustrates that knowing how your opponent plays—tight or loose—assists you in eliminating some of the choices. If you don't know how he plays, the elimination process is more difficult. It means starting from a broader base of possibilities, considering loose choices as well as tight ones.

Card reading takes time and mental energy to learn. There are always clues, depending on the development of the hand and knowledge of your opponent. It is the most important skill to master, so don't be lazy. Practice, practice, practice, until you see spots in front of your eyes.

TIP 78

Do not impulsively call a raise. Breathe, count to 10, think, and act logically in a controlled manner.

If being raised were translated into physical terms, it would feel like someone reached across the table and lightly slapped your cheek. If someone did that to you, would you thoughtfully back away, reciting a passage from the Bible? If you're an average player, your normal reaction would be to sling chips into the pot without thinking, proving that no little raise is going to turn you into a scaredy kitten. But we're not actually trying to prove that our hands think quicker than our heads—in fact, we want it to be the opposite.

For example, say you're playing hold 'em and raise preflop with a pair of queens, and your chauvinistic nemesis tosses his chips in with an arrogant grin. "Baby," he says, "if I win one more pot from you, I can retire in Maui." *Sizzzz*. Of course you don't have a comeback. What do you say to the opponent who has already bought the air ticket on your dime?

The flop comes 4♥ 7♦ 8♠ and you breathe a sigh of relief. So far, so good. On the turn, you're not happy when a king hits the felt, but you bet with shaky hands and the chips go in all different directions. Your opponent reaches for a handful of chips, and you watch in slow motion as reel No. 1 of your nightmare begins again. "Raise her up!" he says gleefully. You fling your chips in on autopilot, and half of them roll into his stack. "Come to Daddy," he chortles. You're too

Setting Your Own Speed Limit

Speed play is a ploy by fast-thinking players to encourage opponents to react on autopilot. Some players need more time to think than others and shouldn't be intimidated by chips flying into the pot like fastballs. One way to thwart the speed player, even frustrate them, is to break their momentum by slowing w-a-a-a-y down. Just as in basketball, if a particular team excels at the fast break, don't play at their pace—make the team play at yours.

far gone to even consider what hand he would have called your initial raise with. The jackass could have had K-J or K-Q—probably not A-K, because he would have reraised. Or he could have flopped a straight with 5-6, and a frustrating possibility is that he tripped up fours, sevens, or eights. When a player is accustomed to beating you day after day, his standards for calling your raises are lowered, because he just knows he'll find a way to come out ahead.

Be especially aware of potential brain freeze when playing against someone who intimidates you or whom you dislike.

Before the river card even hits, you check blind and he bets. You hardly register that it's an ace when you make a fiery call. The lucky SOB turns over A-Q. Only three cards in the deck could have turned his hand into a winner.

What can I say? You lost control: You didn't consider the possibilities, and you made automatic calls on the turn and river. You were right to call on the turn, but throwing in your bet on the river without thinking was madness. This is an extreme example of what happens when you play on mindless autopilot. Be especially aware of potential brain freeze when playing against someone who intimidates you or whom you dislike.

Reversing the situation in our favor, chauvinistic men who take pride in playing fast often experience a brain shutdown when raised by a woman. If you witness a player's frustration and unthinking, quick call to your raise, finish playing the hand rapidly so there's no chance his brain might regain rationality.

TIP 79

Winners use aggression at the right times.

If you were to ask a random guy who plays poker at home with the boys what he would guess to be women's No. 1 weakness at the card table, he'd probably respond, "They're not aggressive enough." But guys who bar women from their games so they can freely talk about tits and football shouldn't presume to know anything about women who have a passion for poker. They are a new breed who innately understand that going through life like a china doll isn't their cup of chamomile. To the contrary, women poker players have a tendency to go over the speed limit and sometimes play too aggressively at the wrong times.

> "Strong players will sooner raise than call."
>
> —Avery Cardoza
> *How to Play Winning Poker*

To dominate a game, you need to be aggressive. If you don't think you can be the force at your table, look for a game where you can be. But dominating a game doesn't mean haphazardly raising at every opportunity; it means playing your good hands as strongly as possible to knock out inferior hands and give yourself a better chance of winning. You want your opponents to react to your actions, not vice versa. If you often find yourself in a hand where you've turned into a calling station, you're playing like a Bloomingdale's mannequin.

Here's an example of controlled aggression in seven-card stud: You have a four-flush on fourth street and are even money to make your hand. Your exposed cards are the 6♥ and 7♥, and your pocket cards are the 9♥ and 10♥; there is only one other heart exposed on board, and there are no eights showing. Four players are in the pot and you are last to act. The A-3 bets out; two players call with unthreatening boards. An aggressive way to play this hand is to raise with your inside straight and flush draws. On fifth street, if you pull a blank, you can either bet again as a small underdog or take a **free card***.

It is important to size up the A-3 player correctly before raising. He must be a thinker but not so aggressive that he reraises and knocks out players B and C, who have vastly inferior hands. They are easy money and you want them to stay in the pot. It would be a perfect world if the A-3 checked his hand on fifth street if you catch a **rag****, giving you the option of checking behind him.

Playing this hand in this way gives the illusion of being super-aggressive, but actually you've played well within the boundaries of common sense. (What was the outcome? It's irrelevant to the point I'm making, but since you asked . . . you caught an eight on the river and won the pot with a straight. The player with the A-3 said, "I knew I should have reraised you!" Players B and C whimpered like little puppies being taken away from their mom for adoption. They were totally oblivious to your additional chance of making a heart flush and winning the hand. Don't explain! Tell them you had a psychic vision.)

*Free card—**getting an extra card without having to risk additional money.**

Rag—an inconsequential and unhelpful card.**

Being the Force

Opportunities for domination by raising on a draw occur when:
- You are last to act.
- You are close to **even money***.
- Your cards are live versus your opponent's cards (in stud).
- You can be fairly sure you won't be reraised.

Make all your bets with an assured confidence that the chips will be coming back home to your stack. Once you have your opponents worried about what you're going to do next, they will become easy to manipulate.

***Even money—when you have a 50-percent chance of either winning or losing.**

A Texas hold 'em example: Remember your old nemesis from the previous tip, the player who said, "If I win one more pot from you, I can retire in Maui"? The dirty rotten scoundrel is back, but with one difference—you're sitting on his left, giving you the opportunity to be the aggressor when he bets. He limps in middle position; you limp behind him with the Q♣ J♣. The two of you, plus the big blind, are in the pot. The flop comes 9♣ 10♣ 4♥. The scoundrel bets, you detect that the big blind is prepared to fold, and you raise. Your hand is not complete, but you're the favorite at this point. If your nemesis has a hand like A-10, you can catch any club, any eight, any king, a queen, or a jack to make you a winner against his 10s. That's any one of 21 cards, and you have two chances to do so. Mr. Rotten reraises. It is not unreasonable for you to raise again to show him you're not a pushover, and if you don't make the hand on fourth street, you can check behind him. Phew, you've finally slowed him down and taken control. The fourth street card is the 9♠ and he checks. You check right behind him. He chirps like a robin ready to swallow a worm, "Yup, I knew you had nothing," and he fires a bet into the pot when a king hits on the river. *Bingo!* Pause thoughtfully and give him an opportunity to believe he's gotten the best of you again; it will increase his irritation when you say, "Raise him up!" This time he makes an automatic call, and as you stack his chips, you can say, "Maui? A trailer park in Pahrump maybe."

TIP 80

The cards don't know when you are due.

How long has it been since you played the last hand? Buddha himself would admire your patience. Still, don't start feeling like a martyr and thinking you deserve a medal for your extraordinary self-discipline. Those thoughts are actually distracting, and you can become impatient by observing your own patience.

> "Nobody ever knows why one person is lucky and another unlucky."
>
> —D. H. Lawrence
> "The Rocking Horse Winner"

There are exactly 101,002 things you can do while you're in the waiting mode. Well, maybe I'm exaggerating the number, but I'm not kidding about the concept. I've said it before, and I'll say it again: Poker is fascinating whether you're playing a hand or observing the action of your opponents, and you can improve your game by simply watching carefully. Choose a player, and try to learn everything you can about him through the play of his cards before you play your next hand. Make believe you're a spy and the director of the CIA wants a report ASAP on all of this player's activities. It will help direct your mind away from the dullness of folding, folding, and folding.

Each new hand is a new beginning in the same way as each spin of the roulette ball is independent from the last. So don't let the pressure of continuous inactivity build up until a J-8 suited looks like a premium hand in early position.

The cards have no memory. Each new hand is a new beginning in the same way as each spin of the roulette ball is independent from the last, or each throw of the dice has no connection to what fell before. So don't let the pressure of continuous inactivity build up until a J-8 suited looks like a premium hand in early position. Remember, poker is all about making correct decisions, and the most important decision is whether to play your starting hand.

TIP 81

Short-handed games are more emotionally intense than full games and create higher fluctuations.

I have witnessed players who are mediocre full-game players become sizzling dynamite in **short-handed*** situations. In contrast, an excellent full-game player can look like he's been thrown overboard in a short game. Sometimes a full-game player just doesn't get the changed dynamics of short-handed play.

The skills required to beat a short-handed game are far more difficult to acquire. Why else do you see the majority of players flee from short-handed situations and even some fine players sit out when it's five-handed? Most players realize that playing with fewer opponents heightens the risk factor and revs up the emotions. It's a much more personal game. Other players, skilled or not, prefer short-handed situations, because they provide a bigger adrenaline rush.

***Short-handed—technically it's any game with fewer than the full number of players, but there's a sliding scale: Five-handed is more difficult than eight-handed, three-handed is far more difficult than five-handed.**

In a short game, you don't have the luxury of waiting for a premium hand, because you'll be eaten up by the antes or blinds. Being forced to play more hands increases the fluctuations beyond many players' comfort levels. They don't like the roller-coaster effect of going straight up or straight down in a brief period of time. Nor do they want to jeopardize a bankroll hard-earned from full games by coming under quick-fire attacks from aggressive and confident players. I don't blame them; it is gruesome to win 40 top bets over the course of three weeks and then lose all 40 in the space of a few hours. *Wheeeee.*

In a short game, you don't have the luxury of waiting for a premium hand, because you'll be eaten up by the antes or blinds.

The best players have a bigger advantage, because they have finer-tuned poker skills than average players. Plus, short-handed games offer more opportunities to make gigantic errors in judgment. But what's interesting is that the weak aggressive full-game player may have an advantage over the tight-tight player in a short game. Mr. Tightie will still be waiting for his usual premium hand before becoming involved, while the loose player is aggressively betting and continually winning the blinds with any two cards. It's amusing to watch a fish swim away because the game got short, when actually it would be the first time he could play with an advantage.

FLUCTUATION JUNKIES

Some players find a nine-handed game as dull as watching cement dry. They will multitask by doing a crossword puzzle or reading the Sunday *Times* from front to back. But if the game gets short, suddenly their attitude changes and their senses become as alert as those of a trained watchdog. Their passion for action begins to percolate. They understand that now is their chance to possibly double or triple their win rate and make some *real* money, because you gain an advantage only when you're in a pot and outplaying your opponents. Errors opponents make after you fold don't help you at all. Playing in a fast short-handed game is like combining three days of play into one session, which can mean a higher hourly earn.

A short-handed situation offers an excellent opportunity to mix up your game. If you snag a pair of kings, consider slow-playing, because you won't be up against as many draw hands. Semi-bluff more frequently. Be overly aggressive on one hand, and tread passively on the next. If the cards fall right, you can make your opponents dizzy from never knowing what to expect next. It's an adrenaline rush of fun when you win, but when you lose—ouch! Imagine the hurt if your dog packed up his doggie dish and moved next door. It's almost as bad as that.

The most inexpensive way to learn short-handed play is to deal out hands and practice with a buddy. When you feel confident enough to tackle a money game, start out at a small limit, because you'll be less intimidated and the financial ups and downs will be less terrorizing. But you have to be careful not to get in over your head, and also to immediately recognize when your comfort level is jeopardized or your big ego has turned on you and has become your enemy. The goal is to always feel as if you're in command, confident in your skills, and at ease with the swings in whichever style game you choose.

TIP 82

When a maniac is winning every pot with any two cards, avoid the tendency to play too loosely.

It's a fluke when you see Marvin the Maniac win hand after hand with rags, such as 8-3, 9-4, 5-4, and J-7, chomping up good hands like A-K, Q-Q, K-Q suited, and A-Q suited. What is the card goddess up to? Does she have PMS or is she having a flashback to an acid trip in the '60s? Should you play just as loose to teach Marvin a lesson? Of course not, but you can loosen up your game by calling with slightly weaker than normal hands and betting more liberally. However, if you try to run a bluff against him, I advise you to get a series of shock treatments at maximum voltage because—haven't you noticed?—*he calls everything!*

ADJUSTING TO CRAZINESS

I start by teaching my students to play a winning game that will be effective at all limits $10/$20 and above, and in which the number of participants in each pot will warrant throwing small pairs away and playing only high-card flushes. Only after my students have a full understanding of the fundamentals and are ready to play their first live casino game do I teach the basics for adjusting to wild games. Wild games are not the standard at limits above $6/$12, and it's easier to add a variation to correct play than to go back to the drawing board and start all over again.

If you've had the experience of learning by the book and then had to adjust to craziness, you may have wanted to feed that book to a wood chipper. Hands like aces and kings, which play better against fewer opponents, are going to lose with a high frequency if you do not manage to improve them. What you must remember is that when you *do* improve them, you are going to win very large pots because of the number of players who were involved in the action. In wild games you don't always have to throw away your small pairs, because you're getting the right pot odds to play. Any ace with a suited card goes way up in value. When you compare your **outs*** to the size of the pot, if your chance of winning is significantly better than the ratio of the pot size to the bet, then you can call because you're getting good pot odds.

If you've had the experience of learning by the book and then had to adjust to craziness, you may have wanted to feed that book to a wood chipper.

But don't use big pots as an excuse for playing horrible hands. I discovered one of my students playing any two cards before the flop in a $2/$4 hold 'em game. I asked gently, "Are you out of your frickin' mind? What's up?" She said that the helpful guy on her right told her to play every

***Outs**—the number of cards left in the deck that will improve your hand.**

hand before the flop because any two cards can win. Believe it or not, he was giving her what he actually thought was good advice. It's true that you can play a few more hands in a wild game than you can in an average game, but you'd better have a money tree in your backyard if you play every hand.

When you first begin to play low limits, it's going to be frustrating when your carefully learned strategies backfire. You won't be able to isolate your big pair, raise on the come, or do anything fancy, because those techniques are designed for reasonable players. Just play good cards and bet good cards. Just because the insane asylum door is open doesn't mean you have to skip in.

TIP 83

Take advantage of a sequence of hands viewed as a rush.

"I want her seat when she leaves! She's on a rush!" Being on a rush means winning several hands in a row. It's more than being occasionally lucky; it's a phenomenon that appears unstoppable—like a tornado where everyone in sight runs for their lives.

The biggest fallacy in poker is that cards fall in certain lucky patterns and reward specific seats. Believing that is as ignorant as thinking killer whales prefer life at SeaWorld over their natural ocean environment. There is no way to predict a rush of cards—when it's going to start or when it's going to end. But shush, don't tell anyone, because most poker players believe that once a series of wins occurs, it will continue. I've even had susceptible players offer to buy my seat on more than one occasion.

> "Playing a winning rush usually gives momentum to all of the elements of winning play."
>
> —Bobby Baldwin
> *Tales out of Tulsa*

If players perceive you as an unstoppable natural disaster, ride the wave to shore and plunder every chip stack in sight. Steal more antes and blinds, and become more aggressive. But be aware that when the rush stops, so does the illusion of greatness, and don't let yourself lose money because you're still holding on to the belief that you're Neptune's niece.

14

Barefoot and Big-Busted in Cyberspace

Online Poker Considerations

TIP 84

Make certain the online poker room you choose has a reliable reputation regarding payouts.

There are as many online poker sites as players who owe me $20. Well over a hundred. But one site is not as good as the next. Some have better graphics, bigger game selections, more informed customer service, faster payouts, or, alas, no payouts at all. This is why you have to check on the reliability of an online casino before you deposit money. A few of my own preferences can be found on my Web site, poker4girls.com, under "online sign-ups." The games at these sites are fair as they use a random number generator, and all info is encrypted. The security measures may drive you a little nutty at cash-out, but I never get annoyed when a second party is being careful with my money.

Large online casinos generally have sound reputations and lousy customer service because of the volume. But when you're a $5/$10 hold 'em player and can choose from more than 20 games, I don't care if the phone rings 25 times before someone picks up or if the operator says "hello" in Swahili.

Large online casinos generally have sound reputations and lousy customer service because of the volume.

Take advantage of the new player bonus. It's usually 20 percent on your first deposit with a maximum of $100. It will be necessary to play approximately four hours of **raked*** games in order to collect the maximum bonus.

There are ways of finding out which online casinos are legitimate and which have shady reputations. One place to check is the newsgroup rec.gambling.poker (Google it for Web site–based access), or you can check the forum at twoplustwo.com. If someone has suffered a sting, it's posted all over the newsgroups.

Of course, there is also word of mouth. If you have a friend who has had a good experience with a particular casino, consider joining that one. Some casinos offer affiliate programs with a cash incentive to induce their existing customers to act as sales representatives. If that is available, your friend should join as an affiliate, because she will receive a minimum of 20 percent of your rake back in monthly revenue. If you sign up at registration with her bonus code, you'll be tracked as one of her players. The affiliate requirements are listed on the home page of a casino site. Promoting the site to your friends is an easy way to

***Rake—the percentage the house takes out of the pot to cover costs.**

make a little extra money. Once you've become a member, you also can sign up as an affiliate.

All reputable online casinos provide a toll-free telephone number for 24-hour service. Before joining, call the number and ask a general question, such as, "How do I deposit money?" At a minimum you'll learn how quickly you receive assistance.

FUNDING YOUR GAME

My recommendation for depositing money is to open a Neteller account (Neteller is an online funds transfer service). Once you join Neteller, you can instantly transfer funds to or from any merchant Web site that supports Neteller's online payments system, and to or from other Neteller members. The simplest and cheapest (free, actually) way to deposit and withdraw money is eCheck by iGM-Pay. You will need to give the online casino information printed on a personal bank check (the routing number, account number, and check number). There is no need to be reluctant to do this; you are not disclosing anything more than you do each time you pay someone by check. Unauthorized withdrawals are not a concern, as they can be made only at your request after you log on to the secure cashier. But if you're a worry wart, you can also deposit money by Western Union or forward a bank draft.

The process of registering and setting up your account at an online casino and depositing money will be a good test of your patience. If you make it calmly through to the end, you're ready to play poker.

TIP 85

Think carefully before you choose your online identity.

When you register at an online poker room, you will be asked to invent a screen name. Players will consciously or subconsciously react to the name you choose (inexperienced players will read more into it than experienced ones). So take a moment to think about the image you want to portray, because it's very difficult to change an established name without justifiable cause.

WHO SHALL I BE?

Aggressive male names like Conan69, Harley1200, or Brutus may keep opponents from initially trying to run over you. A generic but friendly male name like GoodguyTom or EazygoingEd will likely make others feel comfortable, and you'll be easily overlooked as benign. It's pretty hard to turn an opponent with a name like PleasantPete into a villain, no matter how many times he's check-raised you.

Then there are names that attempt deception through misrepresenting your playing expertise: Playdough, Redchecker, and Riverfolder relay the impression that you don't take your money seriously and you're a passive player. This affords you a short-term opportunity to act in an opposite manner to trip up your opponents. Or maybe you want to convey a cavalier attitude that implies drinking is your first hobby and poker is a distant last. Names such as BarstoolBarney, HitandRun, and Neveready also imply that you don't have the attitude of a serious poker player. Another way of opting for frivolous folly is to adopt a cartoon character moniker like LucyVanPelt, SpongeBob, or DaffyDuck.

It's pretty hard to turn an opponent with a name like PleasantPete into a villain, no matter how many times he's check-raised you.

Some players do not want to be easily remembered and use odd combinations of letters and numbers. If you're one of these, go for a completely random selection, such as, j4y832s57h, 974362938, or eoisxlkadhsie. Two small side benefits of a combination of letters and numbers, besides the increased difficulty of recall, are that it's frustrating to chatters because they can't type your name quickly, and it offers no evidence of any personality.

DO YOU WANT TO DISTRACT?

What if you use a trashy name that diverts a man's attention from poker? Names like SpankMe, BelowtheBelt, or Overmoist are going to set male minds adrift and effectively disturb your female opponents by just being icky. Using a name like one of these is a bit like putting a *Playboy* magazine next to a teenage boy while he's working on a term paper on Euclid. It's a continual distraction to a horny-minded young man.

There's the opposite tact: AngelFace, Sugar&Spice, and DadsGirl might turn a tough opponent into cotton candy. *Not!* If you choose a name that's clearly female, you are more likely to be bombarded by an aggressive opponent. If you have aces every hand, you'll relish the advantage. But when you have K-Q and the board comes 9-8-3 and your opponent check-raises your cutesy butt, is he check-raising because he has a quality holding or because he thinks you're a patsy? Personally, I would eschew such names simply to avoid the extra mental baggage.

To keep your opponents guessing, my suggestion is to select a name that is unisex, ageless, and doesn't reveal a geographical location—for example, names like Rebound, Frontrunner, or Monkeyshine. Some players, even expert ones, get distracted by an unknown X-factor. Plus it's entertaining to attempt to chat like a male and not get busted. (It's not an easy task to talk like the opposite sex, so you probably *will* get busted if you're a Chatty Cathy.)

The savvy pro will not be bluffed by your screen name and will rely on your play to determine your experience level and expertise. Yet, who knows, there may be a slight edge in choosing a name that tickles or gnaws at the subconscious of an unthinking or average opponent. Who cares if the observant pro finds you as transparent as Saran Wrap? If one out of six players is tripped up by 2much$ and believes you're a lunatic who wants to give away cash, it is worth planting a decoy.

"Nicknames stick to people, and the most ridiculous are the most adhesive."
—Thomas Chandler Haliburton

TIP 86

Online poker can magnify different leaks in your game.

It's possible to play at least twice as fast online as you can in a live game. If you're a losing player, that means you lose your money twice as fast. Plus, you have the opportunity to play multiple games and "everybody's doing it," so why not you? I'll tell you why not in upcoming tips.

Ten seconds can seem like an eternity online when you're waiting for some goofball to finish the last bite of his bologna sandwich. In live games when someone has called "time," you have the opportunity to entertain yourself by checking out the 7-foot-tall hunky guy who just walked in and is signing autographs (not to mention improving your game by studying your opponents). The casino atmosphere gives your five senses a push-ups-and-jumping-jacks workout, because there is so much stimulation. But online there is nothing to do but stare at an icon and become bored and miffed at Mr. Rude and Mrs. Slowpoke. So you pick up *Fitness* magazine, turn on an old episode of *Chicago Hope*, and order a pizza—all at the same time. Nobody is going to waste 10 seconds of your life. Well, honey, you're already

Ten seconds can seem like an eternity online when you're waiting for some goofball to finish the last bite of his bologna sandwich.

wasted, because now your attention is diverted every which way but financially up.

Online poker is definitely more boring than live poker, although it's technically faster. So there are tons of ways you can multitask: pay the bills, reorganize your sock drawer, change the batteries in the smoke detector; revamp your New Year's resolutions to exclude being patient and disciplined. A mediocre player may get easily distracted. Online poker takes *more* discipline and self-control than live poker, because it's possible to do so many things at once.

Another reason a mediocre player might play worse is that there is no built-in preparation. To get to a live game, you have to make a conscious decision to play. You have to wash up, get dressed, feed the dog, lock the house, and get into your car and drive to a casino or card club. But you can sit down and play a hand of cards online anytime, night or day, to get a gambling fix. I once woke up at 2 A.M. to pee and couldn't make it back to bed without stopping for just one hand of cards. I was still playing just one more hand until the coffee pot switched on at 9 A.M. You always think you can play for just 10 minutes, but when is that really a good idea? When you play poker on the same screen as you play hangman, it's easy to treat the game with little respect.

PLAY MONEY

Mediocre players are inclined to lose touch with the consequences of gambling beyond their means. When you physically don't have to buy in, it's easier to ignore the fact that the next click is two days' worth of wages. There's no feel to the chips, and there's no going into your wallet, so money becomes an abstract concept. Because of this difference, you may chase too many hands or try to overpower your opponent in hopeless situations. You don't have to pay the price of being embarrassed at the hand's end, because no one can see you. I once lost $11,000 in a fast heads-up game, and later when I checked my balance, I was absolutely certain the software had registered my buy-ins incorrectly. When you click for more money, make a notation of how much you've bought to save yourself from postgame shock and fear that the online casino suffered a software malfunction. Put a Post-it on the side of your screen that bluntly reminds you that this is *real* money. When you quit for the day, always check your balance; compare the number when you log on the next day. Online software mistakes may not happen often, but they do happen. So keep a log of what time you started, the limit you played (even the name of the table), and your quitting time. It gives you more authority when dealing with customer service if an error does occur.

Put a Post-it on the side of your screen that bluntly reminds you that this is *real* money.

If the strong point of your live game is intuiting your opponent's holding by reading his body language, you're out of luck on the Internet. Online poker doesn't offer the crafty little ways to run around the mathematical aspects of the game to get clues that live poker does. You need strong card-reading abilities, as well as the ability to determine whether a call is warranted by the size of the pot.

Get out a sheet of paper and make lists of what you think your strong and weak points are regarding your game. Is playing online going to magnify your flaws? Are you really a good short-handed player, or should you limit yourself to full games? Do you get too emotional? If you do, you have a shorter recovery time online because of the speed of the game. It is much easier to become resentful of the table bully and attempt to challenge him.

If right now you are staring at a blank sheet because you don't know what your strengths and weaknesses are, you need to think more about your game in an honest way. Every poker player has strong and weak points, whether she's a world-class champion or sitting at a free-money instructional table. It's time to get introspective and think, think, think. It didn't hurt Winnie the Pooh, and it won't hurt you. Online poker is deceptive and challenging. You can never let your guard down regardless of how well you perform in live games.

TIP 87

Do your homework on your opponents.

When I first started playing online, I "met" a woman in an online poker room nicknamed Trueheart. She was from Bled, Czechoslovakia, and was respected as the best player on the site. I was intrigued by how a woman halfway around the world had gained such refined skills. Inside the chat box I asked her to e-mail me, and we struck up a private correspondence outside of the poker room. When I relayed to her that I was frustrated with my results after my first month of online play, she answered with a two-page e-mail pointing out every substandard play I had made. That was my first realization of how a player becomes an online force. She had developed a digital database that gave her immediate reference to her regular opponents' inclinations. Trueheart was working 20 times as hard as I was, because she wasn't playing with her cat to avoid boredom. She was analyzing every starting hand her opponents played, from what position; the frequency of bluffs and of calling a raise; good or bad calls on the river; aggression or passivity levels; frequency of play; and so forth. Literally in a split-second click, she could pull up a file faster than an FBI agent. I was blown away.

You don't have to create your own database, because software programs are available that will automatically keep track of your statistics and those of your opponents. Simply Google poker-tracking software. At the minimum keep dated alphabetical references in a notebook that you can easily refer to when you sit down. Read up on your opponents before you ante (or blind), and familiarize yourself with their playing styles. Be aware that players' games improve over time, so don't rely totally on a dated note that says, "Never bluffs." The times may have changed.

At the minimum keep dated alphabetical references in a notebook that you can easily refer to when you sit down.

On some sites it's possible to click on a player's name and pull down a notepad. After playing one hand with a previously unknown player, you should type at least five observations onto that pad. Don't be a computer-chair sluggard; if you're serious about your game, work steadily on learning everything you can about your opponents' playing habits.

One big advantage of online play over live games is the ability to track your opponents' skills actively versus in a notebook hidden in your lap. If knowing that many of your opponents are keeping tabs on you surprises and alarms you, get cracking on taking your own notes—start by adopting a playmate for your cat.

TIP 88

Bluffing is not as effective online, plus you're more likely to get bluffed.

If a bluff has one out of five chances of working in a live game, it has one out of 10 chances of being successful online. My advice is to be more prone to try a bluff when you have the additional information that your opponent is capable of folding. Inexperienced players usually call, and maniacs just want to see the hand if they have any hope of winning. On the flip side, because there is a greater chance of being bluffed online, call more liberally on the river unless your opponent is rock solid. Observe the pot odds and act accordingly. For example, if the pot contains $240 and the bet is $40, you need to be right only one out of seven times to break even. Anything better than that and you make a profit.

Bluffing is less effective online for many reasons. Among them:

- Players don't have to make any physical effort to put in the chips. With one quick click, the curious cat knows what's in your bag.
- Bluffing is more likely in high-speed games because players' moods are more volatile and they will attempt to outplay you with any mood shift. Players who are scared to bluff in live games suddenly become braver online, because they are hiding behind an icon.
- Players do not suffer any face-to-face shame after a failed bluff. In a live game you'd fall victim to giggles or sideway glances at the table for an insane bluff, but online there's nothing but a chat box that you don't have to read.
- When an online player's stack is dwindling, there is a greater chance that he will fall into an automatic state of "I just don't care" and dissociate from the value of his money. Making or calling a bluff is automatic for a gloom-and-doom player.
- Because of the high speed, players are more likely to react on auto-call. Reviewing the hand takes time away from getting to the next hand.
- Pots have a tendency to grow in size quickly because of the number of bad players on the Internet. Even those players who don't know the difference between pot odds and an English muffin are smart enough to think, What the hell, the chips might fall into my stack with butter and jam.

TIP 89

Learn to adjust quickly from full to short-handed games and vice versa.

Online dynamics change quickly. One minute you're leaning back, making your grocery list, playing ABC poker, waiting for a solid starting hand, and the next moment, the action has dropped down to five players and the bets are flying like shrapnel over a foxhole.

As most players realize, full-game hold 'em and short-handed hold 'em are two different species. If you're waiting for a good starting hand and have to hit the flop to win in a short game, you may as well put your bankroll in a brown paper bag and drop it in the seedy part of town. If suddenly you find yourself in the midst of super action and accelerated speed, don't get your hopes up that your opponents are playing poorly. They're not; they have adjusted to the new dynamics of the game. When you and an opponent both flop nothing, he'll steal the pot. When you flop something, he'll fold. It's literally a no-win situation. Don't challenge strong players; challenge weak ones.

Many players online crave short games. That's why the sites have developed so many six-seated hold 'em games. The difference between a full game and a short game is like the difference between driving a VW Beetle and a Porsche.

But if you're *not* honest about your skill level, you may be traveling 85 mph hour through a school zone and be issued a very expensive ticket. On the other hand, if you're putt-putting along at 25 mph in the diamond lane, you're going to get rear-ended. In both cases you're going to end up with empty pockets after the judge renders his verdict.

Internet games in particular rapidly change from full to short and from short to full. It's highly advantageous and profitable to understand the differences between both styles of play. But if you're the bullied instead of the bully, click and—poof—you're gone without any of the embarrassment of being a chicken.

TIP 90

Do not fall victim to becoming a Chat-Box Cathy.

Sometimes chatting online is an amusing distraction to pass the time. Other times it is used as a means to intentionally cause a weak link to go on tilt. But there are cowards who take it one step too far—those who use the chat box solely for the purpose of unrestrained abuse. The software is designed to censor the most common curse words, but there are many ways that an offensive person—even someone who can't spell "moron" and has a 100-word vocabulary—can communicate disgusting rudeness.

The chat box is most valuable when you use it to gain information about other players that will improve your game against them. For example, Laddie from Belfast seems to be online day and night, and he plays erratically—sometimes well, sometimes like an openmouthed bass. Strike up a conversation with Laddie and say, "Hey, you play pretty darn well when the sun is up." This will start the exchange on a complimentary note, and Laddie will be more likely to be forthcoming and honest. You want to find out how long he's been playing and if any other members of the household use his computer. If you say, "Hey, you play pretty darn well for a young'un," the use of "young'un" reveals something about you (like that you've probably viewed the original episodes of *The Andy Griffith Show*). Be sure your phrasing is subtle, and try to glean information through a series of gentle inquiries so as not to tip off your opponents to your true motivation.

Be sure your phrasing is subtle, and try to glean information through a series of gentle inquiries so as not to tip off your opponents to your true motivation.

Using the chat feature to vent your anger is childish and shortsighted. If you say, for example, "Was your mother a donkey?" you've revealed yourself as an emotional player who's apt to go on tilt. Even worse, if your opponent does play like a hee-haw, why insult him and risk the chance that he'll blink off to another game or another site?

Use the chat feature to gauge a player's emotional state. For example, if a player is a ticking time bomb who types endless strings of misspelled F-words, exploit his frustration.

Don't ever sympathize with him or apologize for any play. Keep him leaning in the same direction, and all his future plays will be predictable. Many players claim that an error in judgment was due to alcoholic inebriation. If a player confesses to this, keep watching. He could be lying, but maybe he's not, and it's good to know who is heading for a PUI (playing under the influence).

If a good player is chatting away amicably, it indicates he's in a stable mood. Don't go overboard in lengthy interchanges with MrGoodMood—if you keep him entertained, he'll likely keep playing well because he won't be bored.

As in live poker, players love to provide reasons why they played a hand in such-and-such fashion. Encourage them. That's all valuable information that increases your advantage over the loose-lipped justifiers.

The chat feature should be used only to entertain the fishes so they stay in the game, or to gain information. If you find that you're incapable of restraining yourself from post-hand expletives, turn the chat off and curse at the computer screen like a normal person.

TIP 91

Be aware of online tells.

The most glaring tell online is when a player's focus is scattered among multiple games. You can check this by cross-referencing the player lists for similar-limit games. If you see the same name in as many as three games, you've found the most predictable player online. He will react like an unemotional robot by folding, calling, or raising on autopilot. Trickiness is not usually part of his playing formula, because he never gets bored. He's going to wait for the best hand and play straightforwardly. A raise doesn't mean anything other than "I've got a very good hand, maybe even the nuts." If your monitor is large enough to pull up both your table and his second game, you can observe when he's playing two hands simultaneously. If you are contemplating a raise, *raise*! He's looking for an excuse to fold on one screen so he can concentrate on the other. You get an extra bonus if he can't get back to his hand quickly enough, time runs out, and his hand is folded. That's one more incentive to bet after he checks. Always liberally steal the blinds or antes of a multiple-game player.

Another blatant tell is when a player uses the pre-action buttons, which respond faster than if a player waits his turn. Players who click ahead of time are generally done with their hands and ready for the next deal. When no more than four players are in the pot and all three of your opponents have used pre-action checks, you can try to steal. An automatic raise, especially by a multiple-game player, indicates a very strong hand. If a player has constantly used the pre-action buttons and suddenly stops to ponder, he may be trying to trap you.

If a player has constantly used the pre-action buttons and suddenly stops to ponder, he may be trying to trap you.

Because the tell is so revealing, even to weak players, don't use the pre-action buttons yourself. If you think the other players won't notice, you are underestimating the correlation between speed and strength. Can you use the tell to your advantage? Yes, you could work the tell in reverse, but I still prefer that you make each action consistent from hand to hand.

REVEALING BUY-INS

The amount of a player's buy-in also communicates his state of mind. If he blinks into a $5/$10 hold 'em game and plops down $42,000, it most likely means that he has taken a series of beats and needs to see his entire bankroll as a visible affirmation of his skill. If you're a chat-box manipulator, you can tickle the underbelly of his fragile ego by saying something like, "Are you trying to intimidate us with how much you can afford to lose?" I'm not happy to see a large bankroll, because it means that the owner is a winning player and has the emotional edge that a comfy green cushion provides. But watch to see whether he comes in flailing aggressively because players have been known to lose their entire bankrolls, especially if they've stepped up a few limits in a desperate attempt to recover a lower-limit loss.

In contrast, if a player buys in with an odd amount like $423 and the software standard is $800, he probably is perilously close to broke. Now is the time to fly like a vulture over his small, mauled stack. Don't give him an easy ride when he tries to limp into the pot on the first hand; raise and put on the pressure. Many players with a short stack are beyond the hope of recovery and are almost willing to mail you a check for their remaining chips. He won't back down from a raise because he's past caring, and he may become annoyed and raise you right back with a pair of ducks. If you are playing stud, your board shows four hearts, and he raises you on sixth street, he might just be saying, "Please take the rest of it. I just want the merry-go-round to stop." He's going to be unpredictable and illogical, so don't make any good **lay-downs***. If he wins the hand and clicks out of the game, so be it. You had a great **overlay****.

TIP 92

A reasonable amount of paranoia in relation to collusion is a good thing.

There are several ways I know of (and probably several I don't know about) to cheat at poker online. So let's all get paranoid for a moment to think about them. The simplest and most obvious scenario is two creeps, one in Minneapolis and the other in Duluth, playing at the same table using Instant Messenger or Ma Bell to tell each other what they're holding. If one has kings and the other has aces, the kings will drop out. That will harm you if you are playing a flush draw in which multiple players provide better odds. High-handing is hard to detect if you're

*Lay-downs—the act of folding your hand after deciding you're beat.
**Overlay—a bet at favorable odds.

> "I cheat my boys every chance I get. I want to make'em sharp."
>
> —William Avery Rockefeller

playing in the game, but it's easy to detect if you're working for the casino site and monitoring the hands played. Good sites do have people monitor the action and check for the frequency of strange occurrences. But so many hands are played on the larger sites that cheaters can accumulate a lot of money before getting booted off.

HAM SANDWICH

A more aggressive way to cheat is for two players in collusion to sandwich the second-best hand in the middle of a raising war. For example, Phlegm has queens, you have 10s with an ace, Slimeball has junk. Phlegm bets, you call, Slimeball raises, Phlegm reraises, you call, and Slimeball reraises, and so forth until your hand has the smell of 14-day-old gym socks. On the river Phlegm bets, you call with 10s and your stupid deuces, and Slimeball mucks because he never had a hand at all. Phlegm shows queens and fives. You never get to see Slimeball's hand and are left scratching your noggin, wondering what on earth he was so excited about.

If the two cheats become greedy and try this stunt frequently, you'll catch on darn fast that they're making a condiment out of you. This play can also be detected easily if the hands are being monitored by the casino. If you suspect that you're being cheated, write down the hand number, quit the game, and alert the casino staff by phone or e-mail that you'd like the hand history reviewed. You actually have more recourse online than you do in a live game to have the players permanently ejected.

UNDERHANDED INSTITUTION

Sometimes the casino itself cheats. It uses hyped-up software to generate more action that favors the weak player and can destroy the experienced player. For example, in seven-card stud, the software can generate three players all starting with three-of-a-kind. A second scenario is one player being dealt pocket kings, another pocket queens, and a third pocket aces. These are extreme examples, but I have played on a site where two players flopped a flush. The probability of one player flopping a flush is 0.84 percent; the probability of two people flopping a flush is 0.49 percent. I didn't see this happen once; I saw it three times in the same afternoon. In another triple play, in the space of one hour, three times I was dealt a pair of aces, only to be beaten each time by three sixes from the same opponent. I wanted to make a submission to *Ripley's Believe It or Not*. There's no way to ascertain whether a casino is artificially creating action except to use common sense. If you're an experienced player, you'll have the history for making comparisons, but if you're inexperienced, you may think everyone starting with a high pair is normal. In effect, your viewpoint becomes slanted.

Sometimes a casino uses hyped-up software to generate more action that favors the weak player and can destroy the experienced player.

MAN OR MACHINE?

The newest scare is the development of "robots." To keep their games filled or just to make more money, online casinos have allegedly developed "bot" software. The purported robot has been fed playing situations of all types and taught to play each situation as close to perfectly as possible without taking the human variant into account. Of course, it's possible for very smart players to develop this software themselves and switch on the program, go to the video arcade, and come back and count their winnings. When I first heard the rumor about bots, I thought, my heavens, what else is possible in the world of technology? But I also suspect a conspiracy of this magnitude would be difficult to cover up—there would just have to be too many people involved. Or would there? One reason I try to have at least a brief chat with an expert online player is to eliminate the possibility that she is a bot. I do note in my record books if a player has never responded to any of my inquiries. It might mean high-tech fishiness or it might just mean the player doesn't speak English. Do I believe bots exist? Yes. Have I any solid proof? No.

> "When I told Canada Bill the game he was playing in was crooked, he said, 'I know it is, but it's the only game in town.'"
>
> —George Devol
> *Forty Years a Gambler on the Mississippi*

If you know several fine players who are not winning at a certain site, don't try to break the streak. That's one good reason to ask players online what their win/loss stats are; they might fib, but some may not. If you learn that a player you respect is a lifetime loser, it's time to scoot to another poker room.

All that said, sometimes we suspect cheating and there isn't any. You have to remember that there are far more bad players on the Internet than in live casino games. We may get miffed that we got sandwiched and look for someone or something to blame other than ourselves. Plus, we all want a concrete reason for continuous bad luck, especially one that doesn't involve us not being as good as we think we are.

You can't play effectively under a cloud of fear. Obsessive thoughts of the icon next to you being a robot or a crook will detract from your game until you turn yourself into a loser. It's easy to change games if it becomes clear that SeattleSal and BeirutBarry log on at the same time each day. Being on the alert for cheaters is another reason to give the game your full attention, stick to playing one game instead of several simultaneously, and keep detailed notes of unlikely coincidences.

Now let's exit the land of paranoia. I wouldn't write a chapter on Internet gambling if I didn't think there was a good chance you could be a winner by playing fair and square. I've saved the most important Internet tip for last—don't fast-forward your eyeballs.

Murky Morals

One thing that bothers me about Internet play is that some players who would never cheat in a live game cheat online. If they can't see their opponents, in their minds a different set of ethics applies. It's sort of like a normally honest person stealing cable with a black box. I have heard casino players unabashedly brag about cheating online. Their rationalization is that everyone is doing it, so if I don't cheat, I'm just a chump. But a person who cheats has turned into someone much worse than a chump.

TIP 93

As an online player you'll need more discipline to avoid self-destructive gambling habits.

My name is Cat Hulbert. I am an online poker junkie. How come no one else showed up at the meeting? Well, I'll talk to myself until someone arrives with the donuts and coffee. I may know more about the destructive habits of online poker than any professional player. I've had carpal tunnel syndrome from nonstop mouse-clicking. I've played four games simultaneously, gone past my stop-loss limit by a factor of 10, failed to show up for Thanksgiving dinner (and I was bringing the turkey), played in short-handed games when I was outclassed, folded a full house on one screen and raised with 7-2 on the other, and slammed the front door on friends who showed up for an intervention. My telephone answering machine overflowed with so many messages that I unplugged it, my hair

I've played four games simultaneously, gone past my stop-loss limit by a factor of 10, and failed to show up for Thanksgiving dinner (and I was bringing the turkey).

went gray because I couldn't break away to go to the hairdresser (and that was really scary), and I ate my earthquake rations for more than a week because going to the store a half-mile away seemed like a walk across the desert barefoot.

"Once I lost ten blue chips to a player who bet me that the pale light we happened to notice filtering through the curtains was dusk, not dawn."

—Dick Miles
Lowball in a Time Capsule

I was forgetting birthdays and doctor appointments. I let my gym membership expire, and I ate so much delivery food that my neighbor thought I was having an affair with the Chinese delivery boy. One week my mother threatened to change her will if I didn't call. And then she did the next week when I still hadn't called. There was month-old chocolate syrup stuck to my kitchen counter. I was recycling paper plates and drinking coffee out of Pyrex bowls. I developed the same aversion to the sun as Dracula. The blinds in my house were always drawn to cut down on computer glare. But I asked myself, "Who was I hurting?" It wasn't like I was robbing 7-Elevens in a Nixon mask to support my heroin habit, right?

Then the electricity went out for two days. I got the jitters and the sweats, I had no reason to be awake, and I'd forgotten how to read. My cats hissed at me because my scent had changed. I'd hit bottom and was all alone with my own truths. Can anyone relate?

I kissed off my good buddies in cyberspace who were always trying to bluff and steal from me and went cold turkey for a year. My kitchen got clean (what I mean is that I let the housekeeper back in), I made amends with my friends, and I

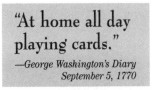

> "At home all day playing cards."
>
> *—George Washington's Diary September 5, 1770*

felt self-righteous enough again to give advice. I broke off my nasty relationship with the Marlboro man and started to attend writing classes at UCLA. I began playing poker in the casino again and rediscovered my force as a player. And yes, phew, I got my hair colored so I was no longer afraid to look in the mirror.

HEED MY WARNING!

If you take up poker online, it can be as destructive to your life as you think it is fulfilling. It can deteriorate your live poker skills by causing atrophy in your ability to read facial expressions. It can turn you into an antisocial hermit with a chronic backache who ignores clocks—and the bathroom scale. You *must* monitor yourself and play only when you are bright, alert, and sitting at the computer to make money instead of feeding an addiction. The first time you blow off a commitment to play, you need to reestablish the borders between your real life and your cyberspace life. Be careful, be very, very careful that playing doesn't begin to take the place of things that are really important—like time with your loved ones, reading, being creative, and watching *ER*. I play online for a living now, but in the same professional way I do as a live-game player. I sit down prepared, I don't multitask, I play only one game at a time, and I heed my stop-loss. I also replenish my earthquake rations every month. (Just in case the earth does start to rumble.)

15

Honey, I Blew Up the Chips!

Tips for a Smooth Home Poker Game

TIP 94

Mind your manners and keep the game friendly.

As is pretty clear by now, I believe that whenever you play poker, you should try your best to win. But when you're playing poker at home, I assume it will be among friends and that you'd like to keep those relationships on good terms. Even if the home game is among strangers, you still should want to be invited back. Here are some special rules of etiquette for home games that don't usually apply to casino play.

- Don't brag about your winnings. In fact, keep a low-key profile, especially if you're a consistent winner. Your goals are to be happy-go-lucky, have a good time, and be a positive contribution to the atmosphere.
- Some women are eager to give advice at the poker table. *Don't do it.* Nobody likes a know-it-all, and you can easily irk the other players. Adopt the one-player-per-hand rule.
- If you are leaving early, make your intentions clear. Home poker games require organization, and there's an expectation that you'll play for a certain length of time. It's unfair to

take a spot another player could have had if you're planning to stay only a short while. Also, it's good etiquette to give your friends a chance to win their money back. Booking a fast win and taking off can leave sour faces behind.

- Never look at another player's hand during or after the action. Any expression you make can be enough to tip off what she is holding. And don't pick up someone's hand to take a peek after she's discarded—you're gaining unfair information that you didn't pay for.
- Don't moan over your luck or act like a Monday-morning quarterback who bet on the wrong side. Complaining isn't attractive—leave the whining to the boys.
- In games where alcohol flows freely, be prepared to make sure all invitees make it home safely.
- Most important, be reliable. If you accept a poker invitation, be on time and don't cancel on a whim. Unlike your monthly book club meeting, a home poker game requires a miminum number of players, and one person's absence affects the whole game.

TIP 95

Set reasonable stakes.

If you set the stakes too high, some novice players will take a major hit, and you'll eventually lose your game. Be reasonable—no one wants to eat canned mackerel all week to be able to afford Thursday-night poker. Still, the stakes have to be high enough to matter; otherwise, strategies such as bluffing will not be effective. If it takes only a nickel to call a hand, it will be called out of curiosity rather than logic. But if calling requires an amount that is meaningful to you, you will have to consider the possibility that you might lose.

My dentist (possibly the world's best and most expensive) has played poker for years for 25¢/50¢. I chide him about playing with seven other doctors to whom winning or losing $25 a night is as inconsequential as what flavor of toothpaste to use. Where's the risk factor in their game? You have to establish a limit that pinches at least your ego, or otherwise you won't care about the outcome.

But then again, my dentist has a point. Home games are about camaraderie. If you err on your betting stakes, err on the low side.

TIP 96

Plan a method for settling disputes ahead of time.

Don't be so naive as to think a dispute won't occur between friends. The most experienced player should be mutually agreed upon by all the players and designated as the arbitrator for the evening. If the arbitrator is unsure of what the correct decision is, she should come to a logical decision that satisfies both parties. Often hard feelings can be avoided if she can get the players to split the pot.

Some standard rules to settle mishaps:

1. In seven-card stud, what happens when the river card gets dealt face up?
   - If only two players are in the pot, the second player also gets his card dealt faceup and the action continues.
   - If more than two players are in the pot, the remaining players get their cards facedown and the player with the exposed card can decide either to declare herself all in or to continue participating in the action.
2. In Texas hold 'em, what happens if the dealer accidentally turns the fourth card (turn card) up before the action was completed on the flop?
   - The card is placed to the side and shuffled back into the deck after the action on the turn is completed.
3. What happens on the deal if one player is dealt an exposed card?
   - Finish dealing the round and then replace the player's exposed card with the next card off the deck. The exposed card becomes the **burn card***.
4. In seven-card stud, what happens if the low card brings it in and then folds his hand?
   - That hand will continue to be dealt cards until there is a bet.
5. What happens if a player bets before it's her turn?
   - The action backs up to the player whose turn it is. The

***Burn card—the dealer takes the top card off the deck, "the burn," and places it facedown under a chip in the pot between dealing each round of cards.**

player who bet out of turn is not bound by her previous decision.

6. What happens if a player calls a single bet when in effect it was a raise? Can she take her single bet back?
   - If there was no action behind her, she can take the bet back.
   - If there was action behind her, she is obligated to either call the raise or muck her hand and forfeit her single bet.

TIP 97

Elect one player to be the bank president, and keep all other hands off the vault.

This tip is for home games that use paper money buy-ins and convert to chips. The first home game I hosted for my students taught me a very important lesson. When you're cashing out and the till is short of money, who's responsible for the payoff? That's a decision that should be made ahead of time. To avoid errors, only one person should be in charge of the bank, and she should be competent with arithmetic—and ideally sober. The best method is to keep a record of money exchanges on paper. When a person buys in, jot down her name and how much she bought. When she cashes out, have her initial the sheet next to how much money she received. Discrepancies don't have to arise because someone was intentionally trying to cheat the till; it could be that a player simply forgot she was paid (as in my first game).

To avoid errors, only one person should be in charge of the bank, and she should be competent with arithmetic—and ideally sober.

TIP 98

As always, be honest.

Cheating on your boyfriend is a misdemeanor; cheating at cards is a felony. Integrity is a big part of poker.

I was once invited to a home game where Happy Harry always seemed to get an ace when he needed one. Have you heard the expression, "He's got an ace up his sleeve"? Well, Harry literally did. On a previous deal, he would **hold out*** a card from the deck and save it until he needed it to make a hand on a future deal. Happy Harry wasn't so happy when he was asked to leave and didn't receive a cash-out for his chips. It's wise to occasionally count down the deck to be certain all 52 cards are in play. Who knows, the queen of clubs may be stuck to the bottom of someone's roast beef sandwich.

Another embarrassing moment occurred in a home game

***Hold out—a way of cheating in which a player removes one card (or more) from the deck for later introduction.**

when Bad Luck Louie **splashed the pot*** when calling a bet. What Louie did was short the pot intentionally, saving a $5 chip. It was bad luck for Louie that I have an eagle eye when players toss their chips directly into the pot. Believe it or not, some players will put the exact amount out when they extend their hand, but when they withdraw their hand, have **palmed**** back part of the bet.

Some players concentrate so hard on making two pair that they overlook the possibility of making a flush or a straight. If a player shows a winning hand but doesn't realize it and mucks her cards, and the pot is pushed to you, correct the error. You wouldn't be cheating by taking the money, but I would think less of you if you did.

> "At the card game, one of the boys looked across the table and said, 'Now Reuben, play the cards fair. I know what I dealt you.'"
>
> —Lyndon B. Johnson

One instance of "dishonesty" (in the loosest sense of the word) that I witnessed was between two very close friends. Jane knew her friend Laura was bluffing on the river. Instead of Jane keeping her mouth shut, she kept adamantly coaxing Laura's opponent to call. Jane was so insistent that I thought she was going to put in the money herself. What was Jane's motivation for hoping Laura was caught bluffing? Jealousy is the only answer I could come up with. Poker does reveal the best and the worst in people.

***Splash the pot—throw chips into the pot as opposed to placing them neatly to the side.**

****Palm—a cheating maneuver in which a chip or a card is removed from the table by concealing it in the palm of a hand.**

Sometimes the most unlikely person will be guilty of intentional cheating, even in a small-limit home game. What can she be thinking to risk her reputation among friends for a few dollars? Sad. Just don't assume everyone has the same ethics you do or is even capable of living up to yours. If you find out something you didn't want to know about a friend, you have two choices: damnation or forgiveness. If she is a valuable friend, you may want to give her a second chance. That's your call.

TIP 99

Never call out what hand possibilities another player has showing.

Try to resist pointing out your opponents' hand possibilities, such as, "Uh oh, someone could have a flush," or "Josie needs an eight for a straight," or "Sarah lands a cowboy." This is the kind of thing people do in sitcoms, and I hope your game is a little more serious than *Friends'* Rachel borrowing money from Phoebe and Monica to raise Ross on the river.

Even more annoying is the player who makes noises of regret after she's folded and a card that would have helped her hand is dealt. This can completely ruin the representation of another player's hand or destroy the possibility of anyone executing a bluff. Who cares what you folded? You no longer have the hand, and it's therefore irrelevant.

TIP 100

Wild-card games decrease the role of skill and favor the weaker players.

I may as well say it from the start, because you'd detect my feelings anyway: Wild-card games aren't real poker. I put my nose in the air at Follow the Queens, spit on Baseball, and see red at The Man with the Ax, One-Eyed Jacks, and Deuces Wild. It's true that each player should have the option of calling her own specialty when she deals, but she should select a game that doesn't take four people to figure out the holding when the cards are turned over. Rule of thumb: If no one has written a book on how to play the game, don't allow it in the lineup. Let's get serious—you're never going to be a good card player if your game of choice is Ting-a-Ling.

Let's get serious—you're never going to be a good card player if your game of choice is Ting-a-Ling.

TIP 101

Don't berate your opponent after a hand, regardless of whether you won or lost.

Never chastise another player with comments such as, "My hound dog has more card sense than you," or "It's uncanny, the more you play, the worse you get," or make any derogatory remark on how a hand is played. It's her money; she can play any way she wants. Plus, if you think about it, you will realize that you'll have a better chance of ending up with her chips if you don't draw attention to her bad play. Yes, sometimes it's frustrating when you have aces and 10s, and she has jacks with an ace and catches your ace on the river. But if you have to Krazy Glue your trap closed to restrain yourself, do so. Criticizing another player only makes you look like a sore loser.

It's equally important to be a gracious winner. Don't gloat when you're stacking your chips. Remember, next time you could be walking in her Jimmy Choos.

TIP 102

Loaning money can be hazardous to a friendship. Try to avoid it.

I'll bet that 80 percent of the people reading this book can name at least one friend who owes them money. And how do you feel about your friend today? How does she feel about you? Is she calling you each day saying, "I'm working on getting you paid off"? Chances are that if you have resources your friend views as more than sufficient, she will rationalize you don't need the money, and at the minimum you will go to the bottom of her creditors list. If you happened to lend her the money while playing cards, she may convince herself that you should have known better than to loan her money when she was emotionally vulnerable. And if you happened to win the loaned money—hey, she'll think, you already got paid back!

It's better to refuse the request right off the bat and risk temporarily hurt feelings than possible long-term damage to the relationship.

It's truly a no-win situation. If you say no to lending money, there will be hard feelings. If you say yes, you may feel irked if she makes an unnecessary purchase while you're waiting to get paid back. There is a rule at Hollywood Park Casino in Los Angeles that none of its employees may loan money to the casino's patrons, because the customers will be less likely to come back. The same goes with friends. If they owe you money, it's less likely you will hear from them. It's better to refuse the request right off the bat and risk temporarily hurt feelings than possible long-term damage to the relationship.

16

Please, Thank You, and, By the Way, Your Fly Is Unzipped

Rules of Etiquette

TIP 103

Show respect toward other players and yourself.

Does poker reveal a person's true colors? I have often heard players remark about a friend on a tirade: "He acts like that only at the poker table. Outside of here, he's actually a nice guy." Can that really be true if the guy just intentionally threw the cards in the dealer's face or made a remark so racist that even an HBO censor would cringe? I once witnessed a dealer's boyfriend wing the cards at her knuckles after he lost a hand. Her eyes began to water,

Sore Losers

Good feelings have an expiration date when you're on a losing streak. When money, emotions, and pride begin to boil in the same pot, the reasonably mannered Dr. Jekyll can transform into the psychotic Mr. Hyde. At some point, most everyone suffers a behavioral meltdown at the table that is accompanied by later embarrassment. This is forgivable once if you learn something, but is unacceptable if you don't and outbursts become habitual.

but she understood that although he may have kissed her good-bye when she went to work, he couldn't control his loathing because the last card she dealt wasn't in his favor. He holds the status of being one of the top players, so this behavior is especially disturbing and shameful.

Fight off your negative feelings as hard as you would fight off someone trying to kidnap your child. Or at the minimum, keep them to yourself because, as I've stressed, table image is the No. 1 priority. Your opponents will enjoy your public tantrums, and they'll be quick to take advantage of your emotional state. Of course, we're only human. You *will* get stirred up and you'll feel like cursing, stuffing the cards in your bra and huffing off, or picking up a water bottle and bopping the sarcastic chauvinist on the head. But darling, if you can't manage self-control, get away from the table as quickly as you would if it burst into flames.

GRACE UNDER FIRE

There are two types of card players: those who accept responsibility for their actions and those who blame others. There are temporary advantages and disadvantages to both behaviors, but in the long run if you accept responsibility for playing a hand poorly, you will learn from your mistakes. If you don't, you will continue to perpetuate the same old errors.

While watching the World Poker Tour, I am amazed by the players who are incapable of controlling their emotions, even when they are on national television. Imagine how they act when they're not on TV! But some people are the pictures of grace under fire. I recently observed Lee Watkinson finish second in back-to-back WPT broadcasts, and I

Gender and Blame

Is there a difference between men and women as far as accepting responsibility? My observation is that women, who tend to have the weaker self-esteem, are more likely to accept fault. But accepting responsibility out of weakness may turn into self-deprecation, while accepting blame out of strength can be a valuable learning experience. You can always go back to the drawing board if you slip up; the point is to never give up on changing identified flaws.

respected his stoicism as much as his skilled play. The disappointment at finishing second after grueling days of playing poker must have been torturous. But what we witnessed as viewers was the type of man we'd want our daughters to fall for—calm, gracious, with all the attributes of a champion, regardless of being No. 2. Equally admirable is Barry Greenstein, the "Robin Hood of Poker." He is the most charitable and compassionate player on the tournament circuit. When the pressure is on, he plays intensely and competitively but never displays anything other than gentlemanly behavior. Needless to say, not every thought that crosses these players' minds during battle is love thy fellow man, but you could never tell, and admirable behavior is essential to preserving a winning and respect-worthy image.

When you make friends with people in the poker room, gravitate toward the players who respect others as well as themselves. Just say no to whiners, crybabies, and hotheads, because I do think poker shows a person's true character.

TIP 104

Part of your job is to make the casual player's experience enjoyable.

Some poker players don't understand how an intelligent person who plays daily can play the game so poorly. They think smart people should play poker well after years of table time. But this just isn't the case. Most of the top poker players have gigantic brains, but not all people with high IQs can master the art of playing poker. I don't detract anything from, say, a doctor's ability to perform heart surgery just because he sits down at a table and draws to an inside straight. First of all, he may have a lot of cash and be playing loose; second, he may be playing solely for entertainment; and third, maybe he doesn't care if he never becomes a great player. Not all of the people you play poker with will take the game as seriously as you do. These players are our bread and butter, and part of our job is to make their playing experiences pleasant so they will return.

Respect all players, whether they have a chip on their shoulder, are trying to get even from playing poorly in the pit*, want to play big-time poker only because of the recent

***Pit—the area of the casino where games such as roulette, craps, and blackjack are dealt.**

popularity of the game, have some self-destructive need to lose, or best of all just want to have fun. Whatever their reasons for playing, remember that you are the practiced pro, or at least try to act like one. It behooves you to be tolerant and to smile when they accidentally get lucky. If you can't stand players who don't know what they're doing, go play with Chip Reese and Jennifer Harman.

In general, the typical male tourist won't respect a woman's presence at the table and will try to outplay you. You're going to have to show him who's boss, but do so cheerfully. Laugh when you lose, tap the table to indicate "good hand," and make him feel like he's a part of the everyday gang. You will be frustrated if a big-money tourist plops down thousands and loses to Arrogant Al, then to Timid Terry, then to Tom, to Dick, and to Harry, and when finally you get your turn for a slice of the green—damn nag it—he gets lucky against you. Console yourself; at least you lost to someone who is going to keep your money circulating.

OLD ATTITUDES DIE HARD

Let me tell you about an encounter I had with an old-school fish dripping in cash who took an immediate dislike to me. I'm playing $50/$100 seven-card stud at Caesar's Palace when a cigar-puffing, bigmouthed drunk accompanied by two young escorts with uncommon amounts of cleavage (well, maybe not for Las Vegas) pulls up a chair. The other players start to drool. He shoots a disgusted glance in my direction, bangs his scotch so hard on the table that it slops on the felt, and barks like a man who has minions for employees: "Women should sit behind the table. Call the manager! Get herrrr out of heeeere!"

OK, you blowhard bastard, I think, get ready for an education in women's rights. My heart is beating quickly, not from fear, but rather with a boxer's lust to spill blood. Then he throws five $100 bills in my direction, sneering, "I'll give you five hundred bucks to get out of sight!"

Now feeling a need to be just as rude, I ask, "Is that more or less than you offered the ladies behind you to stay in sight?" Then I pick up five $100 chips off my stack and throw them in his direction saying, "The same offer goes for you—five hundred dollars to get out of my sight." I think I won the first round, because the chips flew back at me. I can't quote exactly what he said, but it did have a lot of words beginning with B and F.

The night proceeds, his cigar smoke is gagging, his escorts are yawning, the scotch keeps disappearing, and I just can't latch onto a hand that will sober him up and make him slobber apologies. *Finally,* I peek at my hole cards and discover buried aces. I reach for my imaginary boxing gloves and say, "Raise him," and then fire the chips right in his direction to be intentionally confrontational. I'm not expecting what happens. He gets out of his chair and announces to the dealer: "I'm going to take a piss. Play the hand out. Raise her till she starts to cry." The cretin doesn't even look at his cards.

Respect all players, whether they have a chip on their shoulder, are trying to get even from playing poorly or best of all just want to have fun.

I have $3,500 in front of me, and the raises go back and forth until I'm all in against an opponent who isn't even there. On fourth street I catch a third ace. I feel glee, turning my hand faceup for the greedy-eyed **gallery***. The dealer turns my opponent's hand up, and then I feel it—the no-no of the early gloat. His hand on fourth street is 7-3-9-4, all offsuit. But I'm not going to be heading off to the little girl's room; I have $3,500 on the line against the biggest jackass I've ever played poker with. Blank for me on fifth street, king for him. Blank for me on sixth street, five for him. Uh, oh! The time between the sixth- and seventh-street cards feels like slow motion as the dealer pitches the last card facedown. I don't improve and have only three aces. The dealer reaches across the table and turns up the bastard's last card; it is a six, giving him a straight and the winner. It's a genuine read-'em-and-weep result, as the gallery gasps and laughs. The jokester in the No. 2 seat says to me, "Looks like you should have taken the five hundred dollars."

I can laugh about it now, but back then it took me two hours to accept that I'd lost. Would I do anything differently today? Not in regard to going all in with my aces versus three random cards, but as to the cretin's challenge when he first sat down, I could have said, "I'm sorry, sir, that you have such a negative response to women at the poker table." Nah, that could never happen. I would have choked on those words and had the manager yelling, "Is there a doctor in the house?"

But I do wish that I hadn't made that slur about those uninvolved escorts. They could have been his daughters, after all, as odds-defying as that might seem. Sometimes it's just best to let the cards speak instead of your mouth, and hope you don't run into an inside straight.

***Gallery**—a large gathering of spectators watching a hand.**

TIP 105

Toke appropriately, but don't do so to be liked.

Tipping is part of the poker environment, but if you're an everyday player, you must avoid gratuitous **toking***, especially as a means for being liked. As your dollars dribble away, you may not realize how much of your profit is being divided among the dealers, chip runners, floor personnel, **brush****, cage attendant, porter, waiter (in casinos that serve food), and valet. On average, you will tip $40 per day if you expect to please everyone. If you play five days a week, that's $200 off the top; multiply that by an average of 48 weeks, and you've spent $9,600 out of your pocket for what? In some cases you get better service, but not from the dealers. They remember only players who don't toke. Tipping floor personnel is a type of blackmail. If a floorperson is called to make a decision, he might lean in your favor if you are the tipper, but he won't let that influence him if he is honorable (and we prefer that he is).

The casino industry, like the restaurant industry, has always counted on patron tipping to supplement employee earnings. There's no other way these businesses could get people to withstand the pressures of dealing or waiting on

***Toke—common Las Vegas jargon for tip.**
****Brush—the employee responsible for greeting a patron and adding her name to the waiting list if an open seat is not available.**

tables for minimum wage. As restaurant patrons, we would feel miserly if we walked out of a restaurant without tipping even a bad waiter. The same pressure exists in a casino, with one difference: In a casino, not only staff but also players are observing whether you tip. If you don't reward the dealer for simply doing his job (and you'll get the same service regardless), you'll suffer stares and the bolder players will comment on your stinginess. It's a lot of pressure for anyone to withhold a dealer tip, but for a woman it's more, because—gosh darn it—we need to be admired, even if we have to turn into tipping suckers to prevent a negative opinion.

HAVING IT BOTH WAYS

For the unenlightened, it appears to be only a dollar here or a dollar there. And if you don't play often, it's just that. But if you play regularly and you tip $1 each time a pot is pushed to you, as a low-limit player ($1/$2 to $6/$12) you'll be walking to the cashier's cage with an empty rack, and as a middle-limit player ($10/$20 to $30/$60) you won't be able to support yourself by playing cards unless you live in your car.

It's up to you how generous you want to be (and in general I'm a believer in generosity), but be aware that overtipping can be the difference between being a winning poker player and a losing one. As a five-day-a-week player, if you decrease your tips by just $5 a day, you could still be liked and save $1,200 a year. You won't be known as a stiff, and you'll still get good service and be treated respectfully. One way you can reduce your toke overhead is by not tipping on pots that don't go to the river. Even easier, if the pot is big, tip; if it's small, don't. If you're a low-limit player, tip the floor personnel on a weekly basis instead of daily. I see no reason to tip the cashier at all, because that's just one too many open palms. But these are suggestions for the person who is trying to make a living by playing poker. If you're in the casino just to have fun, sprinkle **red birds*** generously and you'll become a lot of employees' best friend for the day.

I'm running the risk of being very unpopular with casino employees, but maybe the cold facts of how much tipping costs will help them understand why a player has to choose selectively whom to gift with a gratuity.

***Red bird—slang for a red $5 chip.**

17
Nuggets You Won't Find for Sale on eBay

A Few Valuable Miscellaneous Thoughts

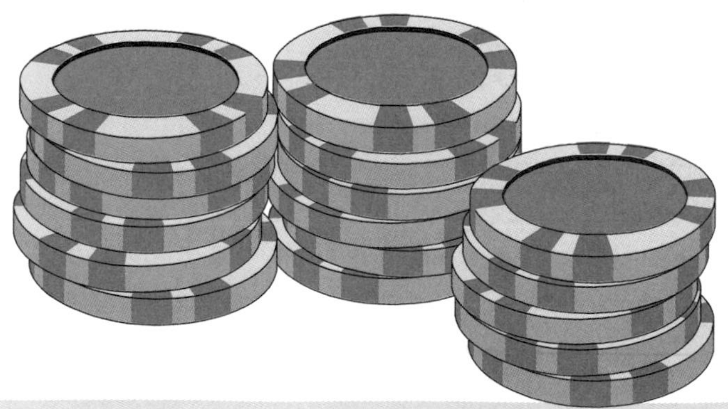

TIP 106

Do not try to learn limit hold 'em from watching the World Poker Tour no-limit tournaments on TV.

No-limit hold 'em and limit hold 'em look like the same game, but they are as different from each other as a stroll is from a 200-yard dash. In limit hold 'em you must stay within the structure of specific bets. In no-limit you can bet as many chips as you have in your stack, which makes it easier to bet players off the best hand by using courageous instinct or by throwing caution to the wind in a moment of impulsive insanity.

At the beginning of the third season of the World Poker Tour tournaments, Lee Watkinson had a dominating chip lead early at the final table. He raised or called most raises before the flop, and regardless of his hand strength, he led out after the flop with a large enough bet to force his opponents who wanted to call to commit a large percentage of their chips. He pushed opponents into folding good hands, as well as drawing hands, because of his proportionately large bets. That's where the gamesmanship of no-limit shows itself—when large bets can force drawing hands or better hands to fold. That does not happen often in limit, where pot odds usually dictate a call.

The show you watch on TV has been edited to provide maximum excitement. The majority of hands dealt at each final table do not make the cut. The ones shown are those with the highest level of drama. In some cases we are watching great poker players; in others we are watching players who will never again get lucky enough to reach a final table. One error in limit hold 'em may have you asking the nurse for a Band-Aid, but one misplay in no-limit can have you dialing 911 for an ambulance.

One error in limit hold 'em may have you asking the nurse for a Band-Aid, but one misplay in no-limit can have you dialing 911 for an ambulance.

Check out this hand that heralded the fatal ejection of two highly successful players. Blinds were $15,000 and $30,000, and the table was six-handed. Alan Goehring was in early position with a pair of jacks and made a minimum raise to $60,000. Doyle Brunson came **over the top*** for $526,000 (all in) with Q♣ 8♦, and Ted Forrest went into a deep think with A♦ J♣. This would appear to be a no-brainer fold for most. But because of his experience playing with Doyle, Ted was certain Doyle was bluffing. The problem was that Ted had less money than

***Over the top—when a player reraises a raise in no-limit hold 'em. Charlene bets $10,000, Pat raises $30,000, and Margot comes over the top for $50,000.**

Doyle, so his call of approximately $500,000, while demonstrating strength with two raises in front of him, only increased Alan's eagerness for making the call (which he did) and potentially scoring a huge pot. Moves like Ted's could easily be deciphered as just that, a "move," and not representative of a stronger hand.

If Alan held a decent pair, there is the possibility that Ted was **sharing some of his outs*** with Doyle. Because Ted had only $30,000 invested in the pot and he would finish sixth to Doyle's fifth if they both were knocked out, his decision to go all in was highly debatable. Sometimes being smarter (having more information) than the third player in the hand is a powerful incentive to take a risk. In terms of pot odds, Ted knew that Alan most likely did not have a hand that warranted calling two all-in bets. He was right again. What Ted miscalculated was Alan's willingess to fold a medium-strength hand. (In a majority of cases, another pro would have folded the jacks without a second thought.)

If Ted had had enough chips to go over the top of Doyle, this would have put more pressure on Alan to fold, and if he had folded, Ted's play would have made him look like a hero. But unfortunately, he overestimated Alan's skill and underestimated Alan's hand strength. Ted and Doyle were both eliminated from the tournament when neither an ace nor a queen hit the board, and Alan won a pot worth more than $1 million.

Although the WPT tournaments are exciting television, you can't see what goes on in the minds of the players. Without knowing every factor that contributes to a player's decision, you can become easily confused by a play that is correct for

***Sharing the outs—needing the same card to improve a hand.**

no-limit but foolhardy for *limit* hold 'em. In limit hold 'em, an A-Q is never going to make an A-K fold for a raise. But it could happen in no-limit if the bet were sizable enough to jeopardize the A-K's chances of survival in a tournament.

Limit hold 'em and no-limit hold 'em may both look like a duck, but one quacks and the other roars.

TIP 107

Be aware that as a low-stakes player, the high rake is hard to overcome.

I have observed that many of my female students are reluctant to raise their stakes. I recommend that as a beginner, you start at the lower limits but actively work toward raising your stakes because of the high rake in low-limit games. The rake is where a casino makes the major part of its revenue. In a $2/$4 game, the rake is typically a $3 maximum, which is higher than in games with higher stakes. It might seem unfair that the rake targets low-limit games, but middle- and high-limit players wouldn't stand for a higher rake cutting into their profits.

To be a winner at the lower limits, you have to be an excellent player and realize that marginal hands earn only pennies. To get better value in relation to the rake and the bet size, your goal should be to play at $6/$12 as soon as possible. When playing in a low-limit game with opponents of equal skill, you'd all go broke in a startlingly short period of time and wonder where the money went. Into the casino's coffers, that's where!

TIP 108

Play, play, play. There is no substitute for experience.

On average I have played 28 hours of poker a week for 15 years. One hour of poker is approximately 30 hands dealt × 28 hours × 52 weeks × 15 years = 655,200 hands I've paid to see. Is that enough to say there will never be a new hand recorded in my mental data base? Nope. The completed puzzle is never the same because the personalities involved in each hand are always reshaping the pieces involved.

You cannot learn how to play poker by only reading about or watching the game. It's like reading 100 books on sailing. Would that make you a seaworthy captain if you've never been at the helm? You have to participate actively to understand how to navigate, maintain the boat, and not get lost in the Bermuda Triangle. Book knowledge offers a good foundation, but you have to be at the tables, making the split-second decisions to understand the depth of the game. Most important, you have to like having your butt in the chair and eagerly anticipating the next hand.

> "The next best thing to playing and winning is playing and losing. The main thing is to play."
>
> —Nick "The Greek" Dandalos

When you first start playing, you might wonder what is so difficult about this game. Why all the hoopla, analysis, pages written on the subject? If you think the game is easy, you are giving yourself credit for being a Navy Seal when you've only snorkeled across shallow water. Only through practice will you appreciate the depth and the risks of diving in over your head without an oxygen tank. One session at a time you'll gain new insights, improve your skills, and learn how to breathe underwater. Steady as she goes.

TIP 109

Don't associate with rattlesnakes.

There will be players with white hats and players with black hats at the table. It'll be clear to you through their behavior and the talent they display who are the ethical girls (and guys) and who are the bad hombres.

Be selective in your friendships. Even if the black hat is a fierce player and is trying to induct you into his gang, stay on the same side of the street as the sheriff's posse. You get to mold your reputation only once, and being associated with the undesirables may stain your image permanently.

If anyone ever suggests that you should cheat together and offers the rationalization that everyone is doing it, don't fall for it. Stay away from him and future games he sits in. Be on the lookout for players who show up in his game consistently in the future, and you'll be able to figure out who he convinced to be his accomplices. It's the rule of the Old West: Good people hang out with good, and bad with bad. However, I wouldn't necessarily advertise that the outlaw sought you out. You never know if your divulgences will have unfortunate repercussions.

Cheats are a fact of life in casino and Internet card rooms, but they are a minority not worth becoming paranoid over.

TIP 110

Think about poker away from the table.

Relive your poker games when you're in the shower, when you're doing dishes, when you're driving to work. Think about the players you encountered, the dynamics of your interactions with them, how the game differed from the one before. Consider your own play from the vantage of an outside critic. Is there a player who is still reading you like an open book? What pitch can you throw that will finally strike him out? Are you still making that wearisome mistake of playing past your stop-loss? Why is it that you have to make one gigantic boo-boo before you realize you're tired? I'll bet there's one hand you fumbled through that if you had known how to play it correctly, you would have. Who can you seek out to help with the answers?

If you're really into the game, you'll be following this advice naturally. The list of things to analyze and review is as long as the time you've spent mucking hands and waiting for action.

TIP 111

When leaving a casino, stay on the alert for non-players watching you cash out.

I wish it weren't so, but as a woman, you are vulnerable to being followed home and robbed. You are more likely to be noticed and watched as a female player, because you are still somewhat a novelty—especially at the high-limit games. Increase your peripheral vision to include the area surrounding the table and the bystanders on the rail. If someone is lurking around and you just feel he's out of place or that he has a motive for watching, other than fascination with the game, don't be shy about requesting management to ask him to move.

Unlike Las Vegas casinos, many casinos in other cities are located in the seedier parts of town. There is a higher likelihood of crime, and you need to be aware of who is watching when you cash out. If you're a small-time player, you might think thieves wouldn't bother with you, but they might have other things on their minds besides stealing your $100. When driving away from a casino, always keep an eye on your rearview mirror and check out the car behind you. Become suspicious if you slow down and the car does too, or if you make an odd turn and it stays right behind you. Know the location of your local police station and drive directly to it if the coincidences start spelling trouble. *Always* have your cell phone turned on and in your lap in case of an unexpected emergency.

I have actually waved my player's deposit receipt in the air after I have cashed out to send the signal that I'm not carrying any cash out of the casino.

If you are a high-limit player, you are especially vulnerable. Do not flash cash at the table. If you are in a questionable part of town and you go on a winning streak, convert your chips into a larger denomination rather than stacking them up to the sky. Most casinos cater to the high-limit player by supplying a player's bank or a secured room with safe-deposit boxes. Use that room and be obvious about entering and exiting it. I have actually waved my player's deposit receipt in the air after I have cashed out to send the signal that I'm not carrying any cash out of the casino.

If you are a high-limit player, install a security system at your house. If you are a single woman, this is mandatory. Be cautious, stay alert, and don't ever believe something bad couldn't happen to you.

18
The Yellow Brick Road Doesn't End at Oz

Keeping the Big Picture in Mind

TIP 112

Derive your well-being from your execution, not from your results.

Sad, but true—as you become more experienced, you'll never feel as happy about winning as you feel miserable about losing. As you become a better player, you'll start expecting to win. It's like a woman who receives a diamond necklace on each wedding anniversary. With necklace No. 1, she showers her husband with kisses. At necklace No. 5, she starts to get a little blasé: "Thanks, darling. Now can you walk the dog?" On their 10th anniversary, her husband goes into her jewelry box and takes three of the necklaces and hocks them. Although she is still left with six diamond necklaces, she's miserable at the loss of her previous fortune. It's human nature—we take for granted what we have, but we are devastated when it's lost.

> "If you win, and you're not excited, then you haven't won at all."
>
> —John Gollehon
> *A Gambler's Little Instruction Book*

You will inevitably lose the special thrill that you initially felt at winning, but you will never lose the sense of well-being that comes from excellent execution. That's where you should concentrate your post-session emotions—on how well you played, not on whether you won or lost.

TIP 113

Foster friendships with good players.

Poker doesn't appear to be a lonely activity, but it is, especially when it's you against a table full of men who share a common goal—they all want to win your money. If you can look up from the table and see even just one friendly face that hopes your ups are way up and your downs are short-lived, it's like hearing James Taylor sing, "Don't you know, you've got a friend . . ." when you need it the most. The more your friend is able to empathize from direct experience with what it's like to lose a rolled-up hand on the one hand or to make a brilliant bluff on the other, the more comforting she'll be when things

Having poker friends is the difference between a solo roller-coaster ride at night and riding with someone who will share the ups and downs of the adventure.

are in turmoil, and the more she'll be able to share your joy when everything is coming up roses.

Value the friend who can stop looking at his own cards long enough to listen to your bad-beat story without yawning. Having poker friends is the difference between taking a solo roller-coaster ride at night and boarding the car with someone who is willing to share the ups and downs of the adventure. But remember, having a good friend always starts with being one too. There are right times to seek help and right times to offer it.

> "A gambler's acquaintance is readily made and easily kept—provided you gamble too."
>
> —Edward Bulwer-Lytton
> *Pelham*

FIND A MENTOR

Like teachers, experienced players often want to share the knowledge they've acquired, and some are willing to mentor a fledgling player with potential. No one has been luckier in that regard than me. I've had the opportunity to learn from some of the best players in the world. Some players are good without knowing why they play the way they do; others (and these are the ones who make great teachers) can explain why and when a specific play is called for. They have a sound mathematical understanding of the game but also a philosophical approach intertwined with psychological insights. Shower appreciation on players who share their wisdom. If you're lucky enough to make long-lasting friendships with them, they may both guide you through the dark tunnels and shine light on your game.

TIP 114

Don't let your passion for poker turn into greed.

What's wrong with longing for boundless wealth? After all, don't Heather Locklear, you, and I all deserve the very best? Aren't we worth it, just like the L'Oréal commercial says? But there's a problem in poker when the desire to earn evolves into greed. Greed demands to be satisfied immediately, and in poker good play may not be rewarded today, next week, or even this year. To play excellent poker, you need a mind free of clutter, one that's patiently detached, almost indifferent to the results, not one that's filled with gnawings of more, more, more. You need extreme patience and a long-term outlook.

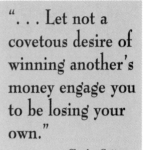

> ". . . Let not a covetous desire of winning another's money engage you to be losing your own."
>
> —Charles Cotton
> *The Compleat Gamester*

Greed is harmful to the soul. It's hard enough to ward off ill feelings against your fellow man after you've been pounced upon, ridiculed, tricked by fate, and humbled by the hundreds of hands where the outcome is beyond your control without adding greed into the equation. There is no justice in poker, and it requires the endless practice of acceptance. If greed is guiding your motivation, you will be a very unhappy person, stuck with feeling endless desire without fulfillment.

Erosion of the Soul

You don't want poker to change your essence. Over the years, I have watched too many players' exuberant expressions turn into stony resentment. Some players cannot prevent negative feelings from creeping in when they are struggling, and others appear to have fortunes drop from the sky. The randomness of luck defies an explanation but demands acceptance if your attitude is going to remain free of the destructive fallout of envy. I'm assuming you are a kind person, and if you find that poker is affecting your outlook on whether the good people outnumber the bad, take a new head count and you'll likely find that you've let the few bad apples ruin the barrel.

TIP 115

Never become lackadaisical about your game—or your life.

Regardless of what stakes you play ($1/$2 or $1,500/$3,000) or the skill level of your opponents, there is always room for improving your game. Phil Ivey, a five-time finalist on the World Poker Tour, who also plays in the world's highest-limit poker games, told an interviewer that he's still actively working on improving his game. The admirable skills I can glean from watching his performances on television are that Phil has unfaltering concentration, intense powers of observation, and the temperament of a monk. He stays in the zone. It's obvious that he loves poker.

When your zest for the game is high, poker is also fun. When it stops being fun is when your skills start to disintegrate. Are there any other ventures in your life that have stopped being fun? Perhaps tending your garden, fixing up your home, getting your doctorate, writing your novel? If you think about it, it will likely become apparent that when it was still fun, you were energized by it and performed with more insight and creativity. It's natural that after you've engaged in the same activity for a long time, some of the initial spark will diminish. But the question you want to answer is, is the activity truly becoming dull or are you just becoming lackadaisical about it?

I doubt if you will ever play a session of poker during which you don't learn something about the game or yourself, unless you're playing on automatic. Auto play often befalls poker players with battle fatigue; those who have lost their passion for the game. When you are playing on automatic, everything about your game, from picking up tells to evaluating distinctions between hands, begins to fall apart. You may once have been an excellent player, but you'll soon turn into an average one who can be manipulated by the players who still love analyzing the full spectrum of the game.

If you can recognize this happening, try to rekindle your enthusiasm. That may mean going back to square one and reviewing your poker readings and notes. It's a challenge to start thinking about the game from a new perspective, but I guarantee that there is a way to reconsider an old point and learn something new from it. If something has meant a lot to you in the past and you are meant to continue the endeavor, you will find a way to rediscover the excitement. Otherwise you'll have to settle for mediocrity. And as short as life is, why settle? Steve Jobs recently said in his commencement address at Stanford University that he looks at himself every morning in the mirror and asks, "If today were the last day of my life, would I want to do what I'm about to do with my day today?" He goes on to say that if the answer is no too many times in a row, then he knows he has to change something in his life. My viewpoint is, either work hard to get the verve back in whatever you're doing—whether it be poker, romance, writing, your job, sports, anything—or put your thinking cap on, review your talents and interests, and point yourself in a fresh direction that you will find fun and personally rewarding.

If something has meant a lot to you in the past and you are meant to continue the endeavor, you will find a way to rediscover the excitement.

TIP 116

Achieve a balance in your life outside of poker.

It's a paradox that to become a great player, you need to think constantly about the game and play, play, play. But if you don't balance poker with other activities, you can become one-dimensional, lost in the green-felt forest. It actually helps your game if you have activities you devote yourself to besides poker, for example, volunteer work, playing a sport, gardening, writing, cooking, taking classes, and so on. It isn't healthy for a person to become so narrowly focused that at a party if there weren't a poker player there to talk to, she'd be a wallflower. It's a big world out there with issues that are a hell of a lot more important than making two pair. Seeing the big picture helps you come back to your small poker environment and not take yourself so seriously.

There's a poker joke that addresses the topic of poker players putting all their focus on one egg. Try not to become part of the punch line.

> People with a 170 IQ pontificate about the intrinsic energy resident in quantum subspace.
> People with a 140 IQ debate over the symbolism of food in James Joyce's *Ulysses*.
> People with a 105 IQ discuss whether it's the fuel injection or the carburetor that needs replacing.
> People with a 70 IQ drone on to anyone who will listen, "I had aces in the pocket . . ."

I happen to think this joke is very funny, but I often think things are funny that others don't. Of course I don't believe poker players have low IQs (quite the contrary), but I do think we have the tendency to become insular in our profession because of its obsessive nature. If you were one of those people who didn't hear about the tsunami in the South Pacific until a week later because you were staring at 52 rectangles of plastic, your life isn't just being lived in a pond—it's being experienced in a puddle.

TIP 117

Adopt a dog. You get extra credit for adopting one from the pound or a rescue organization.

If you are a canine lover like myself, you already know that having a dog as a companion can lift your spirits, regardless of how much money you lost or how many mistakes you made. A dog loves you simply because you were smart enough to find your way home. And the fact that you can open a refrigerator door heightens your status to genius. Coming through that front door at night and encountering the bubbling enthusiasm of your four-legged furry friend will turn any bad day into a good one. It's impossible to stay depressed when you feel so loved and appreciated.

> "Much has been written about the loyalty of dogs, but what I love about them isn't so much their devotion to me so much as their devotion to being alive."
>
> —Steven Bauer
> *Take That, Will Rogers*

Plus taking your dog for a walk is good for you—it reduces stress, it stretches your limbs after a long day in the chair, and it helps clear away the cobwebs of self-condemnation. A one-session loss (for most of us) seems inconsequential when you're outside under the sun or stars with your pal who gets as excited about seeing a squirrel as you do about hearing the words, "Take it." Would you have taken that mind-clearing walk if it weren't for Sparky?

To a woman, a dog is far more than her best friend; the relationship is akin to being rescued by a handsome prince who not only promises to love you forever, but actually will.

Appendices

1. Go to Bed with the Pros

2. Know the Lingo

3. Learn the Key Odds

4. Know the Rules

APPENDIX 1

Go to Bed with the Pros—Recommended Poker Reading

Take an expert to bed with you. I don't mean literally hop in the sack with the authors; I mean with their books! Avail yourself to their years of hard-core experience and hard-earned wisdom. Start with a light kiss and work yourself up to hard-core reading. Here are some of my favorites.

Intermediate Stud

Seven-Card Stud for Advanced Players
by David Sklansky, Mason Malmuth, and Ray Zee

Advanced Stud

The Elements of Seven-Card Stud
by Konstantin Othmer

Beginning Texas Hold 'em

Hold 'em Excellence: From Beginner to Winner
by Lou Krieger

Intermediate Texas Hold 'em

Middle-Limit Hold 'em Poker
by Bob Ciaffone & Jim Brier

Inside the Poker Mind: Essays on Hold 'em & General Poker Concepts
by John Feeney and David Sklansky

Advanced Texas Hold 'em

Killer Poker: Strategy and Tactics for Winning Poker Play
by John Vorhaus

Hold 'em Poker for Advanced Players
by David Sklansky and Mason Malmuth

Poker Books for All Levels

The Psychology of Poker
by Alan Schoonmaker

Zen and the Art of Poker: Timeless Secrets to Transform Your Game
by Larry Phillips

Caro's Book of Poker Tells
by Mike Caro

Caro's Fundamental Secrets of Winning Poker
by Mike Caro

APPENDIX 2

Know the Lingo— A Glossary of Key Terms

Action 1. The liveliness of the game measured by the frequency of bets and raises; if the players are making big pots, the game is said to have good action. 2. If someone says, "The action is up to you," then it's your turn to make a playing decision.
Giving good action means playing a lot of hands; it's not how much you put out on the second date.

Advantage Having the best of it. Same as edge.
"If Mike didn't think he had an advantage in the game, he'd sit out until a sucker sat down."

All in Putting all your chips in the pot and no longer being able to make future bets.
"I only had $5000 in chips, and the blinds were $1000/ $2000, so I moved all into the pot with a pair of sixes."

American Airlines A pair of aces.
Coined, of course, because two aces together look like the airline logo.

Ante A prescribed amount posted by all players before the start of a hand.
If you've never heard someone ask, "Who didn't put up his ante?" you've never played seven-card stud.

Baby A small card—deuce, three, four, five, or six.
"I started with an ace-baby flush draw and lost to an ace-ten."

Backdoor flush When a player was not attempting to make a flush but inadvertently caught perfectly.
"The only way I could lose is if Sarah made a backdoor flush by catching two running diamonds."

Bad beat When a strong hand is beaten by a very weak hand.
Players seek relief from their misfortune by telling bad-beat stories. Tune them out.

Bankroll Playing funds. Shortened version: BR.
Do not hang your purse on the back of your chair, or your bankroll might change hands while your attention is elsewhere.

Bicycle The nickname for the specific hand A-2-3-4-5 (the lowest possible straight).
This straight is also called a "wheel."

Big slick An ace and a king as your hole cards in Texas hold 'em.
"I was dealt big slick and the flop came A-K-K giving me kings full of aces."

Blank A card that does not improve a hand. "I caught a blank."
A seven-card stud example: Your starting hand is A♥ K♥ Q♥. The fourth street card is the J♥. On fifth, sixth, and seventh streets you catch three unrelated cards that do not improve your hand. These disappointing cards are called "blanks."

Blind A mandatory bet for the two players to the left of the button. There are usually two blinds: a small blind and a big blind.
A blind is so named because you put in your money before seeing your cards.

Bluff To deliberately bet a losing hand in the hopes that your opponent(s) will fold a better hand.
"I missed my flush but I tried bluffing the pot because Denzel folds too much on the river."

Board The "board" in stud refers to exposed cards on every street, not just on sixth street. Hold 'em: The five community cards.
"None of the cards I needed to make a straight were on board."

Box The dealer's location when he's dealing, usually heard as part of the phrase "in the box."
"Bonnie has another twenty minutes in the box before she gets a break."

Bring-in 1. In stud games, the amount required to open a pot. 2. Opening the pot with a mandatory bet. "I'll bring it in for one dollar."
Bring-in bets are utilized to start the action and add more moola to the pot. In stud, the player with the lowest card on board has to bring it in. Because seven-card stud favors high-ranking cards, usually the worst hand is forced to join the action.

Brush In some cardrooms, the term for the employee responsible for greeting and seating a patron.
The origin of the job title comes from the employee carrying a brush to sweep off the poker table before a patron took his seat.

Bullets 1. Aces 2. Also chips, because you fire them into a pot like ammunition.
1. My eyes popped open when I saw another pair of bullets in the pocket. 2. Running out of bullets means a re-buy or finding out where the ATM is located.

Buried pair Concealed pair.
A stud player might say, "I started with a buried pair," which means his first two concealed cards were the same rank.

Burn and turn A poker dealer puts the top card of the deck into the discard pile before turning up the next card.
Reason: to make cheating more difficult.

Button The disk that indicates the dealer position.
A player is said to be "on the button" when he acts last.

Cage The area of the casino or cardroom where you can buy or sell chips. Also called the window.
The name came about because the cashier's room is often behind glass or bars.

Call To match a bet.
"I decided to mislead my opponent by only calling his bet, instead of raising."

Calling station A weak player who constantly calls bets and rarely raises.
Note: This is the worst type of player to try to bluff.

Cap In a multi-way pot, it is the maximum number of raises in a round of betting.
"I'll cap it," means that someone intends to put in the final raise. "Cappuccino" is a cutesy way of saying the same thing.

Card sense An intuitive ability to play cards well.
The more observant you are, the more likely you are to have card sense.

Card shark A professional player.
Not the most flattering phrase for an expert player, but it's better than being the suckerfish at the table.

Catch To be dealt the card one needs.
If your opponent sarcastically says, "Nice catch," she's not talking about your new boyfriend.

Check To check means, I do not wish to make a bet, but I will continue to hold my cards.
A player can say, "Check," or use a hand gesture of tapping the table lightly.

Check-raise When a player checks, hoping a later-positioned opponent will bet. When the action gets back to the checker, then he raises.
Check-raising your opponent adds a personal element, because it carries a sting.

Color change Replacing chips of one denomination or color with those of another.
Purpose No. 1: If a player is moving up to a higher game, chips of a different denomination (and color) are often used.
Purpose No. 2: If you've won big, changing your chips to a higher denomination makes for easier transport to the cashier's window.

Come over the top Reraise a raise. Same as "over the top."
Each time Jack raises, Jill comes over the top (maybe to get back at him for making her fall down the hill).

Connectors Two cards in sequence, for example, 8-9.
The odds of making a good hand with off-value cards are always improved when the cards connect. Suited connectors are even better.

Cowboy Nickname for a king.
"Are two cowboys good enough to win this hand?"

Crabs A pair of threes is called "crabs."
If you don't get it, tip them over on their sides.

Crying call Calling a bet when it is likely you are beat. Often accompanied by a verbal complaint.
"There was only a small chance I could win but I made a crying call anyway."

Door card In seven-card stud, the first upcard on third street.
It is valuable to memorize all the door cards of your opponents on third street.

Down and dirty Refers to dealing the last card in stud, because the last card is dealt face down and often determines the outcome of a hand.
You're more likely to hear this expression in home games, because many dealers like to add a touch of Howard Cosell to each round.

Draw dead To draw to a hand that will lose even if you catch perfectly.
If you start with A♥ K♥, and the flop is 7♥ 7♣ 6♥ and your opponent started with a pair of sixes, you are drawing dead to the flush.

Drawing hand A four-card straight or a four-card flush, with more cards to come.
Playing drawing hands, like straights and flushes, is best in multi-way pots because of the odds of making the hand.

Draw-out The best hand gets beaten by a secondary one.
Bad-beat storytellers will say, "I had him until the river, but he drew-out on me."

Duck Nickname for a deuce.
The slang for three deuces is Huey, Dewey, and Louie. Quack, quack, quack.

Edge An advantage.
The more skillful player has a bigger edge in a poker game.

Equity Your expected value in the pot.
For example, if the pot is $200 and you have a 50 percent chance of winning it, your expected value is $100. The phrase is often shortened to just EV.

Even money A 50 percent chance of either winning or losing.
"I don't mind gambling a bit when the odds are even money."

Eye in the sky Ceiling security cameras.
The eye in the sky at the Bellagio Casino has the highest level of surveillance technology in the casino industry.

Face card Any jack, queen, or king.

Queens are also called "girls" or "ladies," and kings are called "cowboys." The poor jack is just a jack.

Favorite The hand that has the best chance of winning before the last card is dealt.
For example, if one player has aces on the turn and a second player has a flush draw, the aces are favored to win.

Fish He who is unskilled and naïve, thus the target of better players.
The fish is also called the "live one."

Floorperson The casino employee who settles disputes and fields requests, such as getting a new deck or calling for a porter, security, higher management, et cetera.
Calling for a floorperson is like hailing a cab: You've got to hope it isn't rush hour.

Flop In hold 'em-style games, the first three cards turned faceup simultaneously after the first betting round.
A common expression is, "I flopped it."

Free card If all players check on a round, the resulting situation is called "getting a free card."
The most common mistake poker amateurs make is mucking their hands when they could check and hope for a free card.

Gallery Spectators huddled around a game.
The higher-limit games draw more poker voyeurs because of high-profile players and mountain-sized pots.

Go South Remove chips discreetly from the table hoping not to be seen.
It's a poker room rule that a player's initial buy-in and all chips won must stay on the felt in clear sight.

Grinder A gambler who ekes out a living at small stakes.
The origin comes from the saying, "Grind out a profit."

Gut-shot The card that is caught to fill the gap in a four-card sequence and complete a straight. For example, if you hold 6-7-8-10 and on the last card catch a nine, you have made a gut-shot straight.
The poker expression "Never draw to an inside straight" (the odds are against you) is as common as "You've got to know when to fold 'em." In both cases, this is solid advice.

Heads-up When there are only two players in a pot.
When the action is one-on-one, there is no limit to the raising.

Hit with the deck Winning an unusually high number of hands.
"Jerry is buying the drinks tonight—he's been hit with the deck all day."

Hold out A way of cheating in which a player removes one card (or more) from the deck for later introduction.
"James got caught holding out and was asked to leave the casino."

Hold over To consistently have better cards than another player.
"When I have kings, Suzie has aces; when I have jacks, she has queens. Every hand we play she holds over me."

Hole card Any one of your unexposed cards.
When peeking at your cards, do so in a way that prevents rubbernecked neighbors from catching a glimpse.

Hollywooding Hamming it up in an amateurish way to attempt deception.
"Joe yawned and acted disinterested during the hand when he made his flush because he was hollywooding before preparing to raise."

Kicker The highest unpaired card that helps determine the value of a five-card poker hand. The kicker often determines who wins the hand when opponents hold the same pair.
"I knew we both had aces, but I was in kicker trouble."

Laydown The act of folding your hand after deciding you are beat.
Caroline complimented me by saying, "Good laydown," when I folded on the river.

Limp in Simply calling the opening bet.
Sometimes this is done for deception; however, when a player says, "I'll limp in," he usually does have a weak hand.

$ Limit Classifications $

What constitutes a high-limit game? When are you playing low? There are lots of opinions on this. Here's my take:

Low limit – $10/$20 and below

Middle limit – $15/$30 through $50/$100

High limit – $75/$150 through $200/$400

Mega limit – $300/$600 through $1,000/$2,000

Ultimate limit – $1,500/$3,000 and above

Live cards Cards that have not been dealt, or at least have not yet been seen.
"Two of my kings were exposed on the deal but I didn't see any aces so my kicker was still live."

Live one A player with very little chance of winning. The sucker in the game. Also called "the fish."
"If you look around and can't find the live one, watch out; you might be it."

Longshot A hand that needs incredible luck to win.
"When Lesley made four-of-a-kind on the river against my queens full I was distressed by her hitting the longshot."

Maniac A player who bets, raises, and reraises without any regard to the quality of his hand.
The psychology of a maniac player is either he has no

respect for money or thrives off the high of acting recklessly.

Muck 1. The discards 2. To throw your cards away. "I mucked the hand."
"I turned over aces up on the showdown and waited patiently for Donna to muck her hand."

Nines up Two pair, the higher pair being nines.
Whenever you have two pair, it is not necessary to tell the value of the lower pair. Simply name the higher pair and add the word "up" or "over." Nines up is used here as an example; it could be any pair, such as kings up, 10s up, sixes up, et cetera.

No-brainer A hand so good that even a bunny couldn't screw it up.
Playing a hand such as four kings is a no-brainer.

Nuts The best possible hand at any given time in a pot.
Do you think it was men or squirrels that made up this one?

Offsuit Cards that aren't of the same suit; for example, 8♦ and Q♠.
Off with the suit has a completely different connotation.

On tilt When you're making irrational playing decisions due to being out of control.
"If I hadn't been on tilt, I wouldn't have tried to bluff the millionaire with open kings."

Outs The number of cards left in the deck that will improve your hand.
"Judy also had an ace, so I had fewer outs than I thought I did."

Overcard 1. In stud, a card in your hand higher than any card showing among your opponents' exposed cards. 2. In hold 'em, cards in a player's hand that are of a higher rank than the exposed community cards.
Never knowingly chase a bigger pair unless your overcard is an ace.

Overlay A bet at favorable odds.
Calling $10 on the river for a $200 pot is an overlay if you have better than a 5 percent chance to win the pot.

Palm A cheating maneuver in which a chip or card is removed from the table by concealing it in the palm of a hand.
"The dealer accused the old-timer of palming a card."

Pigeon A very weak player.
Unlike in the bird world, pigeons are very popular cardroom patrons. They feed us.

Pit The area of the casino where games such as roulette, craps, and blackjack are located.
"Ted was a winning poker player, but he would always go into the pit and lose his money playing craps."

Playing soft Not applying pressure by raising or bluffing.
"At the poker table Suzie and Marvin always play soft against each other, because they're dating."

Pocket Refers to the cards that are dealt face down (the first two cards in hold 'em and the down cards in stud).
The numbskull was playing with a pocket pair of sixes against a hand that had sevens showing.

Pop it To raise.
"Margot was so eager to pop it that she spilled over her drink."

Pot odds The ratio of the size of the pot to the size of the bet a player must call.
If the pot contains $40 and you must call an $8 bet, you have pot odds of 5 to 1.

Producer A bad player with a lot of cash.
"When the producer walked through the door, fifteen players put their names on the list to play with him."

Puppy feet An adorable name for the suit of clubs.
Doggie footprints.

Rabbit hunt To search through the muck to see what you would have made if you had continued to play.
What would have happened doesn't matter if you've folded your cards. Plus, rabbit hunting is against casino poker-room rules.

Rag A card that doesn't improve your hand.
"I had an A-K-Q-J of spades on fourth street, but the next three cards were rags and I lost the hand."

Railbird A player who has busted out of a game and literally hangs out on the railing separator.
"Jerry used to be a high-stakes player, but he went broke and now he's just a railbird looking to be staked."

Raise on the come To raise with an unmade hand before all the cards are dealt with the anticipation of making the best hand.
It's a play that makes you look like a genius when it works, but when it doesn't, there is no consolation prize for a good try.

Rake The percentage the cardroom takes from each pot.
"You'd think the dealer had a piece of the game, he's so anxious to take the rake."

Read To detect the holding of another player using all the available evidence: betting, remarks, body language, open cards.
Most good readers are winning players. Practice whether you are in or out of a hand.

Rebuy The act of purchasing more chips.
"Natalie looked glum as she made her third rebuy."

Red bird Slang for a red $5 chip.
"Neil was always pleased to get a red bird as a tip."

River The seventh card dealt in seven-card stud. The fifth community card in hold 'em.
A player will often say he got rivered by another player,

meaning that he was leading in the hand until his opponent caught a perfect card at the end.

Rock An extremely conservative player who won't risk a cent.
"I am a rock, I am an island, and a rock feels no pain." (Because she's so tight, that's why.)

Rolled up In stud, if your first three cards are the same rank, it's called being rolled up. Three aces is the best possible starting hand.
Talk about an adrenaline rush better than receiving a little blue box from Tiffany. Well, almost.

Rush A streak of winning several hands in a row.
Dealer, keep 'em coming.

Sandbag To misrepresent a good hand with the intention of raising later.
"When Jennifer made trip aces on the turn, she sandbagged by checking her hand."

Semibluff A term coined by poker writer David Sklansky, which means to attempt to bluff with an inferior holding but still have the possibility of making the best hand by the river.
"I tried to semibluff the hand by raising on the turn with four hearts."

Set under set When two players both start with a pair and both flop three-of-a-kind.
The odds of this are 1.02 percent.

Shoot it up To raise.
Poker has cowgirls, too.

Short-handed Technically less than a full game, but the general opinion is that a short game is made up of five or fewer players.
"Johnny is always looking for a short-handed game, because he thinks he's more skillful than the other players."

Shot-taker A player who cheats to win.
"Watch out for Unlucky Louie. The only way he can win is to take a shot."

Showdown The end of a hand when the players turn up their cards to determine which hand wins the pot.
Let it be you!

Slow-play To not raise with a blockbuster hand; waiting till a future time to take the initiative to trap other players.
Generally players who start with rolled-up trips enjoy the deception of slow-playing their hand by only calling a bet or a raise.

Snowmen Two or more eights.
Because that's what they look like (and I hope they don't melt away).

Splash around Betting wildly on losing hands.
"Guy splashed around with so many weak hands he often had big losing days."

Splash the pot Throw chips into the pot as opposed to placing them neatly to the side.
"Scott would splash the pot intentionally to make it impossible to see how much money he put in."

Steal To rob the antes or blinds by raising on a bluff.
"I wish I had the cards to call that steal."

Steam To throw ones money away because of lack of control or emotional upset.
If you're steaming, you'd be better off ironing.

Stop-loss The maximum amount you are willing to lose in one session.
"My stop-loss for $30/$60 hold 'em is $3,000 when I sit down at the table, but when I start to lose, I forget the promise I made to myself."

Street A standard term in stud to designate each betting round.
There will be a third-, fourth-, fifth-, sixth- and seventh-street card. The last card is also known as the river card.

Stuck When you are losing in a game.
A common poker expression is "stuck like a pig."

Suck out Come from behind in a hand and draw out.
Some players are called suck-out artists because they catch the miracle winning card too frequently.

Tap out To go broke and lose all your chips.
"Harry hung on the rail looking for a handout after he tapped out of the game."

Tight A player who has strict starting-hand requirements and who never gambles is called tight.
"Oh great, I just got raised by the tightest player at the table."

Tilt When a player becomes emotionally off kilter and plays wildly.
I went completely on tilt when Suzie cracked my aces, and I played every hand for an hour.

Toke Common jargon for tip.
"Gill was known as a cheapskate, because he never gave the dealer a toke."

Turn In hold 'em, the fourth community card and the third betting round.
"The turn card was an ace, making me worry that someone had outdrawn my kings."

Under the gun Used to designate the first person to act after the low card in stud, or the first player to act after the big blind in hold 'em. (More frequently heard in hold 'em.)
Think about it: Being under the gun obviously isn't a good thing.

Unit Applicable only to limit games. It is equal to the size of the biggest bet.

Some players believe the average win rate is one unit per hour.

Wheel A-2-3-4-5 (also called a bicycle).
KC turned over his hand and triumphantly announced, "I made a wheel on the river!"

Wired pair Starting with a pair.
At the end of a hand you often hear someone say, "I started with a wired pair."

APPENDIX 3

Learn the Key Odds—Some Probabilities You Ought to Know

Knowing the odds is helpful for more than making correct playing decisions. It can increase your patience level if you think an event should happen more frequently than it does, like being dealt a pair of aces in hold 'em or a rolled-up hand in seven-card stud. Plus it can alleviate the disappointment and frustration of not improving enough to win the hand by making something simple like two pair. Odds add reality, and you should definitely learn some key probabilities.

Texas Hold 'em

Pre-flop, the probability of being dealt:
Either pocket aces or pocket kings—1.2%
Any pocket pair—5.9%
A-K suited—0.3%

A-K offsuit—1.2%

(The probability of being dealt pocket aces, pocket kings, or A-K offsuit is exactly the same. If your first card is an ace or a king, then your second card must be one of three specific cards to start with one of these hands.)

Any two suited cards—24%

Any two connected cards—35%

With two unpaired cards, the probability of flopping:

At least a pair (using your pocket cards)—32.4%

Two pair (using both of your pocket cards)—2%

Trips (using one of your pocket cards)—1.35%

With a pocket pair, the probability of flopping:

A set (three of a kind) or better—11.8%

Making a set or better by the river—19%

With two suited cards, the probability of:

Flopping a flush—0.84%

Flopping a flush draw—10.9%

Making a flush with two flush cards in your hand and two on the flop—6.4%

With two connecting cards, the probability of:

Flopping a straight—1.3%

Flopping an open-ended straight draw—10.5%

Making a straight from an open-ended straight draw from the flop to the river—(8 outs) 32%

Making a gut-shot straight draw from the flop to the river—(4 outs) 17%

Seven-Card Stud

The probability that you will be dealt in the first three cards:

Three straight-flush cards—0.14%
Three suited cards—5.2%
Three straight cards—2.3%
Any three-of-a-kind—0.24%
Any pair—16.94%

Starting with a pair, the probability for improvement by seventh street:

Quads (four of a kind)—0.5%
Full house—7.5%
Trips—10%
Two pair—42.1%

Starting with three-of-a-kind, the probability for improvement by seventh street:

Quads—8.2%
Full house—32%

Flush possibilities:

The probability of being dealt a three-flush—5.2%
Making a flush draw on fourth street—20.4%
Making a flush when you are four-suited on fourth street if none of your cards is out—56%. (Subtract 4% for each flush card you can see.)

Straight Possibilities:

The possibility of being dealt a three-straight is—2.3%

The possibility of improving to a four-straight on fourth street—16%

The chance of making a straight by seventh street if all your cards are live—51%. (Subtract 3% from your chances for each primary card exposed.)

APPENDIX 4

Know the Rules—How to Play Texas Hold 'em and Seven-Card Stud

Learning the rules of your preferred/chosen poker game is like starting a shopping spree in a department store. Many of you already have a full drawer of undergarments and can skip the lingerie department and speed on to the outer layers. But for those of you who are bare-bottomed, let's go step by step, going over all you'll need to know to sit down and play for the first time.

THE MECHANICS OF TEXAS HOLD 'EM

Texas hold 'em is appealing to the type of player who can't wait to get to the carnival to ride the roller coaster. The game is fast-paced, and the peaks and valleys occur rapidly, treating your emotions to a wild ride. Hold 'em is full of guesswork, and the better you are at reading people, the more adept you will be at the game.

Basic Rules

For the purposes of this explanation, let's say you're playing a $5/$10 game. The order of play is determined by what's called the "dealer button"—usually a small plastic disk that designates the dealer for that hand. The player directly to the left of the designated dealer posts a small blind bet of $2; the second player to the left posts a big blind bet of $5. They are called "blinds" because players post the bets prior to seeing any cards. The purpose of blinds is to stimulate action.

Two cards are now dealt face down to each player, starting with the small blind and rotating clockwise around the table. The blinds are considered live bets, so the action begins to the left of the big blind on this round only. Each player has the options of:

1. Calling the $5 big blind bet (matching the bet).
2. Raising to $10 (depending on the casino, a maximum of three or four raises is allowed per round).
3. Folding (meaning you toss your cards back to the dealer and are now out of the hand).

When all bets have been equalized, the dealer places three "community" cards face up in the middle of the table. These cards are called "the flop." Community means that everyone uses the same cards on board in combination with her individual pocket (or "hole") cards to create the best five-card poker hand. No matter how good your cards look to you before the flop, if the communal cards don't strengthen your hand or provide a draw (meaning the potential for a good hand), you must be prepared to fold (unless you attempt to

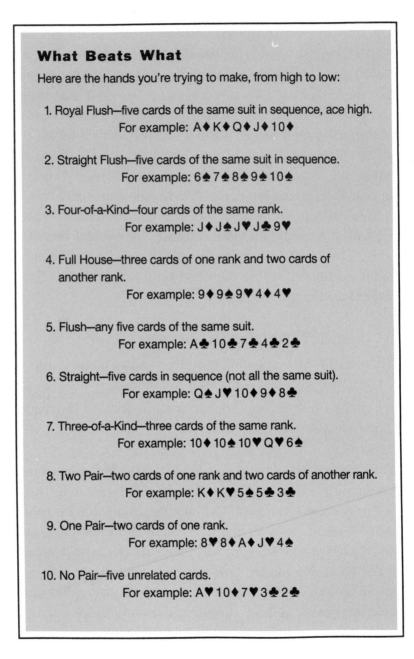

What Beats What

Here are the hands you're trying to make, from high to low:

1. Royal Flush—five cards of the same suit in sequence, ace high.
   For example: A♦ K♦ Q♦ J♦ 10♦

2. Straight Flush—five cards of the same suit in sequence.
   For example: 6♠ 7♠ 8♠ 9♠ 10♠

3. Four-of-a-Kind—four cards of the same rank.
   For example: J♦ J♠ J♥ J♣ 9♥

4. Full House—three cards of one rank and two cards of another rank.
   For example: 9♦ 9♠ 9♥ 4♦ 4♥

5. Flush—any five cards of the same suit.
   For example: A♣ 10♣ 7♣ 4♣ 2♣

6. Straight—five cards in sequence (not all the same suit).
   For example: Q♠ J♥ 10♦ 9♦ 8♣

7. Three-of-a-Kind—three cards of the same rank.
   For example: 10♦ 10♠ 10♥ Q♥ 6♠

8. Two Pair—two cards of one rank and two cards of another rank.
   For example: K♦ K♥ 5♠ 5♣ 3♣

9. One Pair—two cards of one rank.
   For example: 8♥ 8♦ A♦ J♥ 4♠

10. No Pair—five unrelated cards.
    For example: A♥ 10♦ 7♥ 3♣ 2♣

bluff with nothing). If multiple players are in the pot, the rules allow a bet and three raises (in some casinos a bet and four raises). But if two players are heads-up (playing one-on-one), endless raises are allowed.

Unlike the previous round, after the flop the betting begins with the player directly to the left of the button. The options now are to:

1. Check, which means you're not folding, but you're also not adding chips to the pot—it's like taking a pass. You check either by saying "check" or by tapping the table lightly. The action proceeds to the next player. If all players check, the betting round is free.

2. Bet $5.

If someone chooses to bet, the options for the remaining players revert to: **1.** Fold. **2.** Call. **3.** Raise.

One additional play in your strategy arsenal is the check-raise. If you believe your opponent will bet, you can check your hand and then raise your opponent's bet. The upside is you can get more money into the pot; the downside is if she also checks, you get no money into the pot and give your opponent a free card.

When the betting is complete, the dealer places a fourth card face up on board called the "turn card." The only difference in play from the previous two rounds is that the limit now doubles ($10). When the action is complete, a fifth up card (called the "river card") is dealt. After another round of betting, the last player to bet or raise shows down her hand first (if no one bets, the first player with cards left on the button shows down first). After the winner is determined, the button is moved one spot to the left, the player who posted the big blind on the previous hand now posts the small blind, and the player to his or her left becomes the big blind.

Position Is Key

One critical aspect of hold 'em strategy is your position at the table, which determines the order of play. Position is power! Late position is desirable—it is always advantageous to act after seeing what choices your opponents have made. The earlier your position, the stronger your hand should be for you to continue playing. Obviously, if you are on the button (and therefore act last), you are in the best position at the table.

How to Read a Hand

You use the best five cards out of seven to make your hand. You can use both cards from your hand or only one, or you can simply play the board.

Example No. 1

You have A-Q as your pocket cards.

The board reads A♥ 10♠ 3♦ 4♥ 2♠.

Your opponent has 10♦ 9♠.

The winning hand (yours) is A-A-Q-10-4.

You used two cards from your hand, beating your opponent who loses with 10-10-A-9-4. She also used two cards from her hand.

Good Starting Hands Are Like Presents

The most critical decision you'll make is whether to play your starting cards. Be aggressive, but be selective. Any two cards can win, of course, but the truth is that the more you stick with upper-class hands, the less you'll have to resort to asking, "Will anyone take a check?"

Premium Holdings *(small boxes from Tiffany's)*
A-A, K-K, Q-Q, A-K suited, J-J, A-Q suited

Secondary Holdings *(gifts from Neiman Marcus)*
10-10, A-K, A-J suited, K-Q suited, A-Q, 9-9

Third Tier *(24 long-stemmed red roses)*
A-J, A-10 suited, K-Q, K-J suited, K-10 suited, Q-J suited, J-10 suited, 8-8

On the Way Down *(breakfast in bed on your birthday)*
A-baby suited, Q-10 suited, Q-9 suited, J-9 suited, 10-9 suited, 9-8 suited, 8-7 suited

Bottom Floor *(a DustBuster for Valentine's Day)*
A-10, 7-7, K-J, K-10, Q-J, Q-10, J-10, Q-9, J-9

Bargain Basement *(secondhand paperbacks)*
Small pairs (sixes and under), 10-9, 9-8, 6-5 suited

Other pocket holdings are like receiving a roll of paper towels for Mother's Day.

Note: Strength variances may occur depending on whether you are in early, middle, or late position; the game limit; and the number of opponents.

Example No. 2
Your starting hand is 10♠9♠. Your opponent's hand is 3-3.

The board reads A♥ K♠ Q♦ J♠ 3♦.

Use one card, the 10♠, from your hand and play four cards from the board to make a winning straight: A-K-Q-J-10.

Your opponent plays both threes from her hand and loses with 3-3-3-A-K.

Of course, you were both incredibly lucky to begin with to make a straight and three-of-a-kind.

A Sample Hand

Let's join a game in progress and watch some players in action. We're joining them just after the pocket (first two facedown) cards have been dealt.

Hot Pants Helen (on the button) A♦ K♣

Steamy LaRue (small blind) 10♣ 10♥

Cha Cha (big blind) Q♥ Q♦

Bonnie Jean 8♥ 2♥

Flamingo 6♦ 6♥

Annie J♥ 10♦

Lucy 9♣ 4♥

Mary Hartman A♥ Q♠

Judge Judy 6♠ 5♠

The first player to act is Bonnie Jean, because she's to the immediate left of the big blind. She has nothing to think about because her cards are junk, and she *folds*.

Flamingo easily *folds* her sixes. She understands that the chances of flopping another six are only one out of seven, and being in early position and possibly having to act first on the next round is a big disadvantage.

Annie *folds* J-10. Again, this hand is weak and in early middle position.

Lucy, with 9-4, has a no-brainer and *folds*.

Mary Hartman *raises* with A-Q. She has a solid raising hand.

Judge Judy *folds* 6-5 suited. In other circumstances, this hand might be playable.

Hot Pants Helen *reraises* with A-K. Correct.

Steamy LaRue *calls* the double raise with 10-10 in the small blind. Steamy always looks for a challenge. This is a hand that can be rationalized either way for a fold or a call. Some conservative players would fold easily; looser players would see this as a natural call.

Cha Cha also *calls* the double raise with Q-Q. She wants to see how the hand develops before she makes a move.

There are now four players:
Hot Pants Helen A♦ K♣
Steamy LaRue 10♣ 10♥
Cha Cha Q♥ Q♦
Mary Hartman A♥ Q♣

The flop is: K♠ Q♠ J♦

Because the action after the flop starts to the left of the button, Steamy is first to act. Another type of player would feel disappointed, but not overly optimistic Steamy; she sees future possibilities of a straight. She *checks.*

Cha Cha has made three queens. Of course this is exciting, but the board still provides many ways for her to lose, such as someone could have made three kings. In addition, a holding of A-10 would make a straight, and there's also the real possibility of someone making a future straight or flush. She *bets.*

Mary Hartman has made a pair of queens. There are many things going wrong for her here. An overcard has hit the flop (in this case a king), and another player who called a double raise has fearlessly taken over the betting. Common sense should prevail, but it doesn't, and Mary stays involved and *calls.*

Hot Pants *raises* with top pair, top kicker. (A kicker is the unpaired card that goes with a player's pair. The higher ranked the card, the better.) It's the natural play to raise here, but she shouldn't be surprised if a reraise comes right back at her from Cha Cha. Hot Pants' backup plan is a 10 falling, giving her an ace-high straight.

Steamy LaRue unwisely *calls.*

Cha Cha *reraises* with the three queens. There are only two hands that she can't beat, three kings or an ace-high straight. If someone is holding an A-10, she still has the potential to make a full house on the last two board cards.

Mary cuts her losses and *folds.*

Hot Pants Helen knows her A-K is no good at the moment. But she's an optimistic gal, looking for a 10 to make a straight and *calls*.

Steamy LaRue has played poorly so far and sees no reason to be inconsistent now. She *calls*.

The turn card is the 10♠. The board now reads:

K♠ Q♠ J♦ 10♠

There's only one semi-happy camper at this table, and that's Hot Pants, who has made a straight. She still has to worry that someone has made a flush.

Steamy LaRue is still in the awful position of acting first. She has good news and bad news. The good news: She's made three 10s. The bad news: They have a high probability of being a loser. She *checks*.

Cha Cha curses and *checks*. She's smart enough to suspect that Hot Pants Helen has an ace.

Hot Pants Helen *bets* with trepidation because of the three flush cards on board.

Steamy doesn't know the last 10 was folded before the flop by Annie. She is drawing dead (which means there are no cards left in the deck to improve her hand). She *calls*. It's a good thing she has a trust fund.

Cha Cha *calls* with her fingers crossed, hoping for the board to pair on the river.

The river card is the 7♥. The board now reads:

K♠ Q♠ J♦ 10♠ 7♥

Steamy LaRue *checks.*

Cha Cha *checks* with a big sigh.

Hot Pants *bets.*

Steamy LaRue lives up to her name and *calls.*

Cha Cha makes an excellent *fold.*

Hot Pants shows down her ace-high straight and happily takes the pot.

The only player in this hand who didn't make a mistake is Cha Cha. Playing error-free poker doesn't always guarantee that you'll win the pot. But over the long run, you will eventually get rewarded if your opponents make more mistakes than you do.

THE MECHANICS OF SEVEN-CARD STUD

If you have a detective's mentality, an alert mind, and a good memory, you'll enjoy playing seven-card stud. It's like getting a clue with each card dealt, and at the river (the seventh and last card) solving the mystery.

Here's How It Works

Let's assume you're playing a $6/$12 seven-card stud game with California rules, which allow a bet and three raises. Each player starts by posting a $1 ante that the dealer sweeps into the center of the table, establishing a pot.

Cards are dealt one at a time, starting to the left of the dealer. Two cards are given to each player face down (these are called pocket cards), and the third card is dealt face up.

You are now at the point in the game that's referred to as third street. Street is a standard term in stud to designate each betting round. There will be a third, fourth, fifth, sixth and seventh street—also known as the river card.

The first decision you must make is whether to play your first three cards. How do you decide? By evaluating your hand according to the following:

1. Any three cards of the same rank, such as 3♥ 3♦ 3♣, is a superior hand. The best starting hand would, of course, be three aces.

2. High pairs (aces, kings, queens, jacks, 10s) are excellent hands.

3. Three cards of the same suit is a very good hand—the higher the cards, the better. You have the beginnings of a flush. But there should not be more than two cards of that suit exposed in other players' hands (the fewer flush cards exposed, the more likely it is that you'll make your flush).

4. Medium pairs, such as sevens, eights, and nines, are good hands if a card higher than your pair has not raised the pot. But medium pairs generally do not hold up unless you improve your hand.

5. Three cards in sequence, such as 10♣ J♠ Q♦ or 6♥ 7♦ 8♣, are examples of playable hands. But your cards should be live. (If your cards are live, it means you don't see the cards necessary to improve your hand on board.) In the case of Q-J-10, there should not be more than one nine or one king exposed. You need those two specific cards to increase the possibility of making a straight.

Third Street

The lowest exposed card is forced to make a small $2 bet called the bring-in. The reason for a bring-in is to stimulate action and make it more desirable to get involved in the hand, because more money is in the pot. If more than one player has the same rank of low card, then suit in alphabetical order—clubs (the lowest), diamonds, hearts, spades (the highest)—determines who must start the action. Note that the low card can choose to bring it in for a full bet, which in this case is $6.

The player to the immediate left of the low-card bring-in has several options. She can:

1. Fold (meaning you toss your cards back to the dealer and are now out of the hand).
2. Call the bring-in (meaning you add either $2 or $6 to the pot, depending on the action of the low-card).
3. Complete the bet to $6 (if the low-card brings it in for $2).
4. Raise to $12 (if the low-card brings it in for $6).

Note that completing an opening forced bet does not count as a raise. After completion of the low-card bring-in to a full bet, three raises are still allowed.

Depending on the prior action, the next player in clockwise rotation may:

1. Fold.
2. Call the $2 bring-in.
3. Complete (if the bring-in was $2).
4. Raise to $12 (if the bet has been completed to $6).
5. If the pot has already been raised, call the $12.
6. If the pot has been raised, reraise to $18.

The play rotates around the table until all bets are equalized (meaning everyone has put in the same amount of money).

Note: If more than one opponent is in a hand, you cannot raise more than three times on any given street. If the hand is being played heads up (meaning one player against one player), endless raises are allowed. Here's how to think of it—an initial bet and three raises are permitted. This rule was instituted to decrease the chances of being cheated by partners in a game. Hence, in a \$6/\$12 game, with more than two players on third and fourth streets, there never will be more than \$24 bet by any player (except in the case of an open pair on fourth street). On fifth, sixth, and seventh streets, with multiple opponents, the maximum amount will be \$48.

Fourth Street

A fourth card is dealt face up, and there is another \$6 betting round. In stud, the player with the highest cards or best hand starts off the action. This may change with each round, depending on the cards that are dealt. For example, if player No. 1 has A♥ J♥ and player No. 2 has K♦ 10♠, the ace is higher than the king and would act first. But if player No. 3 makes an open pair, that hand is the highest because a pair beats ace high. If two players have the exact same rank of cards, the player left of the dealer acts first.

On fourth street, you generally continue to bet at the lower limit. But if a pair is made, that player may choose to bet at either the lower or higher limit (in this case \$6 or \$12). If that player checks, each player in turn also has the option of betting either \$6 or \$12. If the higher bet is made, all raises must be in increments of that amount. If two players have made pairs, the highest pair acts first.

As mentioned, the person with the highest cards acts first and has two options. She may:

1. Check (which means you're not folding but you're also not adding chips to the pot—it's like taking a pass. You check either by saying "check" or by tapping the table lightly. The action proceeds to the next player in clockwise rotation. If all players check, the betting round is free).

2. Bet $6 (assuming no one has an open pair).

If a player does choose to bet, the next player has three options. She may:

1. Fold.

2. Call the $6 bet.

3. Raise the bet to $12.

Play proceeds around the table until all bets are equalized, then the dealer deals the fifth-street card face up.

Fifth Street

On the fifth card, the betting limit doubles. (So in this $6/$12 game, the lowest possible bet is now $12.) It gets easy from here on, because the rules begin to duplicate themselves.

The highest hand opens the action. If there is a 10♣ 9♣ 8♠ on board versus a K♦ J♥ 4♠, the king-high hand acts first. Once again, if there are open pairs, the higher pair begins the action.

Because you are playing a $6/$12 limit, the highest hand may:

1. Check.
2. Bet $12.

The next players may:

1. Check, if there has not been a bet.
2. Bet $12.
3. Call the $12 bet.
4. Raise to $24, if there has been a bet.

Reminder: All raises on third and fourth streets are made in increments of $6, except in the case of an open pair on fourth street, when the higher limit may apply; all raises on fifth, sixth, and seventh streets are made in increments of $12.

On sixth and seventh streets, betting adheres to the same rules as on fifth street.

A Sample Hand

Let's take a look at a sample hand. The two cards on the left are concealed; the card on the right is exposed.

Starting at third street:

Hot Pants Helen 2♠ K♥ /2♣

Steamy LaRue 10♣ Q♥ /9♣

Cha Cha 6♣ J♣ /6♠

Flamingo J♠ J♦ /10♥

Annie 3♠ 3♦ /A♣

Lucy 4♥ 9♥ /K♠

Mary Hartman Q♠ 5♥ /Q♦

Judge Judy 8♥ A♦ /7♦

Hot Pants *brings it in* for $2.

Steamy, being an action player, *calls* with an inferior hand. Notice that she can see a king, a queen, and a 10 open on board, making her hand fairly dead. (A dead hand means your cards are duplicated more than once on board.)

Cha Cha also *calls* the $2 bring-in with her split sixes. (Split means one card is exposed and one is concealed.)

Flamingo aggressively *completes the bet* to $6 with her buried jacks, even though players holding an ace, a king, and a queen have yet to act.

Annie is not overly excited about her buried threes, despite her live ace overcard, and she *folds*. (An overcard is a card higher than any card showing on your opponents' boards.)

Lucy makes an easy *fold* because she has garbage cards.

Mary Hartman *raises* to $12 with the split queens.

Judge Judy easily *folds*.

The action returns to Hot Pants, who was forced to bring it in with the low-card deuce. She actually has a pair of deuces but chooses to *fold* because her king kicker was duplicated in Lucy's hand, decreasing her chances of pairing her king. (A kicker is the side card that accompanies a pair.)

Steamy LaRue makes another poor decision and *calls* again, adding $10 to the pot.

Cha Cha makes the correct play by *folding* her sixes.

Flamingo *calls* with her buried jacks but doesn't like it. She hopes she will be able to catch another jack on an upcoming street and have a concealed surprise for Mary.

There are three active players in the hand:

Steamy with 10♣ Q♥/9♣ is hoping to catch a jack to connect her cards for a straight draw.

Flamingo with J♠ J♦/10♥ is chasing the queens with the second best pair, jacks.

Mary with Q♠ 5♥/Q♦ is in the lead with her pair of queens.

The fourth-street card is dealt.

Steamy catches the 8♣, improving her chances of making a straight, but she still needs a jack (two of which are concealed in Flamingo's hand). She also has three clubs.

10♣ Q♥/9♣ 8♣

Flamingo catches the A♥, giving her a semi-live overcard to Mary's queens.

J♠ J♦/10♥ A♥

Mary catches a deuce. She still has the best hand, but unfortunately caught a useless card that was duplicated on board.

Q♠ 5♥/Q♦ 2♦

Flamingo, with the highest cards on board, is first to act. She *bets* $6. This is a good bet, because A-10 suited looks scary and she knows Mary is too timid to raise.

Mary tentatively *calls.*

Steamy thinks about raising (which would be a hopeless play), but just *calls.*

The limit doubles to $12, and the fifth-street card is dealt.

Defying the odds, Steamy's fifth card is a jack. She makes her straight.

10♣ Q♥ / 9♣ 8♣ J♥

Flamingo catches another heart, giving her three open hearts on board.

J♠ J♦ / 10♥ A♥ 6♥

Mary Hartman thinks her prayers were answered when she catches another queen, giving her three queens (three-of-a-kind, also called a set or trips).

Q♠ 5♥ / Q♦ 2♦ Q♣

Mary is first to act with the open pair of queens. She *bets.*

Steamy is anxious to get Flamingo out because of her open flush cards (her three hearts), and she *raises.*

Flamingo has an easy *fold,* because she doesn't have a fourth heart for a flush draw and she can't beat the open queens.

Mary hesitates. Steamy could have a straight, but it's unlikely. She has only an 8-9-J on board, and Mary knows she has three of the queens necessary to make one end of the straight. An aggressive player would reraise, but Mary just *calls*. Steamy is loose, but she's not stupid. She knows Mary may well have three queens.

The sixth-street card is dealt to the remaining two players.

Mary is dealt a five, pairing one of her pocket cards and giving her a full house—queens full of fives, which beats a straight by a mile.

Q♠ 5♥ / Q♦ 2♦ Q♣ 5♣

Steamy is dealt a rag (a meaningless card), which is inconsequential because her hand cannot improve enough to beat Mary.

10♣ Q♥ / 9♣ 8♣ J♥ 4♦

Mary is still high with the queens and *bets*.

Steamy throws caution to the wind and *raises* to $24. If she were thinking correctly, she would suspect that Mary might have filled up (made a full house).

Mary *reraises*.

Steamy laughs and *calls*, saying, "I guess you've got this straight beat."

The seventh-street (or river) card is dealt face down.

Mary gets the 3♥. Steamy gets the 6♦. (For both of them, the card they received doesn't matter because their hands are already complete.)

Mary is high, of course, with her open queens and *bets*.

Steamy *calls* quickly, knowing she's probably going to lose.

Mary shows her hand—queens full of fives—and wins.

In this example, the best starting hand ended up raking in the chips. But this is not always the case—she who starts strong doesn't always end strong in seven-card stud.

Who Is Cat Hulbert?

The following is an excerpt from the book Gambling Wizards, *by Richard W. Munchkin.*

In 1996, *Card Player* magazine published an article naming the top seven-card stud players in the world. The only woman on the list was Cat Hulbert. The article said, "It must be emphasized that there is zero tokenism in the selection of Cat. She is that good." And since then, her game has only gotten better.

Prior to her poker career, Cat traveled the world as one of the first female professional card counters. She was a member of the famous Czech team and was part of Ken Uston's group in Atlantic City, where she was arrested more than 50 times for trespassing. Cat became so notorious that she was barred from casinos in Asia before she even sat down at a table. Once, determined to beat casino surveillance, she donned a wig and full beard and took acting lessons to perfect her disguise as a man.

Between blackjack and poker, Cat was also a professional slot player, running a team of octogenarians who sat and pulled handles for her when progressive jackpots reached profitable levels. "Slot machines were the grimiest, dirtiest, hardest work I've ever done," says Cat. "It's the lowest form of gambling you can do." Still, it was good for a few hundred thousand dollars.

Finally, after burning out on blackjack and slots, Cat moved on to poker. She struggled for the first three years, until 1986 when she hooked up with David Heyden and Rick Greider, two of the best seven-card stud players in the world. She took lessons and began beating the game. In blackjack, being a woman had been a big negative. In poker, she found that the opposite was true, as men, with their swollen egos, were easy to manipulate. "No one challenges my authority at the table," she says of her ability to compete with the big boys.

Today Cat splits her time between 150/300 pound online Texas hold 'em, teaching poker for women only at Hollywood Park Casino, animal rescue, and writing. She lives in Southern California.